KITCHEN TABLE
YOUTH MINISTRY
Inviting God to Dinner

KITCHEN TABLE YOUTH MINISTRY

Inviting God to Dinner

JANA STRUKOVA

THE
PILGRIM
PRESS
Cleveland

To my parents and godparents
To Martin and Daniela

In memory of Dušan

Venujem
drahým rodičom a krstným rodičom
Martinovi a Daniele

Na Dušanovu pamiatku

The Pilgrim Press
700 Prospect Avenue
Cleveland, Ohio 44115-1100
thepilgrimpress.com

Library of Congress Cataloging-in-Publication Data

Strukova, Jana, 1970–
    Kitchen table youth ministry : inviting God to dinner / Jana Strukova.
        p.   cm.
    Includes bibliographical references (p.   ).
    ISBN 978-0-8298-1840-6
    1. Christian education of teenagers. 2. Christian education–Home training.
I. Title.
BV1485.S83 2010
268'.433–dc22   2010022480

1   2   3   4   5   6   7   8   9   10   15   14   13   12   11   10

Contents

Acknowledgments

THE THOUGHT OF SPIRITUAL FORMATION happening around the kitchen table came alive to me during a class in religious education at the Candler School of Theology at Emory University. As a postdoctoral fellow in religious practices, I was sitting in class listening to the exchange of opinion between the teacher and her students. That particular class helped refresh images and personal experiences that I had had during conversations around dining and kitchen tables in my own family. My year-long research and teaching opportunity at Candler enabled me to weave the thread of my initial similes and memories into a narrative and a research piece that I now present to you in the form of this book.

I am grateful for the opportunity to have begun to think, research, and write on this topic during my postdoctoral studies at Candler. I benefited greatly from my personal conversations with the professors and graduate students including Carol Lakey Hess, Elizabeth Bounds, Mary Elizabeth Moore, Liz Corrie, and Almeda Wright. I concluded writing this book during my first year at the Episcopal Seminary of the Southwest in Austin, Texas, where I teach Christian Education and Formation. There I initiated more friendships and professional partnerships that helped shape my thinking further. Thanks go to David White, Dori Grinenko Baker, and James Goodmann with whom I had a number of collegial conversations on the subject, gaining more clarity and honesty about my writing vocation.

My own family in Slovakia serves as a source of my formative practices of faith, but also as the source of living memory and examples that I use in this book. My husband, Doug Hume, proved to be a wonderful conversation partner who listened patiently to my thinking out loud and continues to engage and stimulate my thought. I would like to thank my editor Ulrike Guthrie, who worked with my manuscript diligently, kindly, and wisely, trimming the narrative of long or convoluted sentences so that its message could sprout forth with clarity and focus. My research assistants, Beth Wyndham and Diane Pike, compiled the bibliography and provided relief for my tired eyes by painstakingly reviewing all the punctuation in the bibliography and footnotes to make sure it was correctly inserted.

This project is the product of God's call for me to speak and teach God's Word. The people who helped shepherd me through this call are many and their support is manifold. Their support started all the way back in my country of birth, continued through my theological studies in the United States and proceeds now in the context of my profession. I am grateful to all these people who have acted as messengers of God's calling for me. They taught me in words and by example the kind of faithfulness, determination, and life full of divine grace that it takes for one to teach and form children and youth in the Word of God.

Introduction

I WAS BORN AND GREW UP in the former Czechoslovakia. In my faith formation I encountered numerous obstacles, mainly because of the communist political regime and its anti-religion policies. I remember growing up in a climate of fear and uncertainty about whom to trust. My mother raised my brother and me in the Lutheran Church. It was a strange experience. I would attend the worship service, but no Sunday school classes or youth group. There was not much of that going on anyway. Being in the church on Sundays, I felt that this was *the* place where I should not be. What if somebody had seen me worshiping — I mean somebody like a spy who would report my family to the local communist party officials?

My parents would frequently argue about this possibility, with Dad feeling that Mom was opening our family to unnecessary risks such as losing their jobs or losing the opportunity for us to study at a university. It was quite common for the children of clergy or of religiously active families not to be approved by the communist party to study at schools of medicine, journalism, law, or pedagogy. "Politically undesirable" was a category that could easily have been rubber-stamped into our political files and could have altered our professional fates for a long, long time. My mom, who from childhood had learned to conceal her father's origin as part of the intelligentsia, knew all too well the communists' dislike of religion and the educated opposition. Yet she decided not to compromise: She was going to raise us in the church and to educate and empower us to have minds of our own, and so she did.

Central Themes

My personal reflection on how my own family formed me in faith helped give rise to this book and led me to organize it around the following principal themes: family and natural rhythms, kitchen table fellowship, and space.

Family and Natural Rhythms

The Lutheran church in my hometown did not have a strong catechetical ministry (although it did have a two-year long confirmation preparation which I went through). The bulk of my faith formation consequently happened in our family milieu. My parents were not overly devout: we did not pray before each meal, we did not read from the Scriptures every day, and we did not even attend church every Sunday. Our spirituality was not extravagantly visible, but it was subtly present in ways that were not imposing, yet perhaps the more inviting for that. Mom's Bible, hymnal, children's Bible stories, and devotional readings were neatly stored in her bed stand, and I remember the image of her reading from them every evening. I remember my grandmother singing songs from the hymnal, and me joining her in my off-key but genuine way. I remember walking to the church on freezing winter mornings, three of us pacing swiftly to generate some body warmth, perhaps not talking the talk of faith but instead literally walking it through the unplowed snowy streets.

My tapestry of spirituality has been woven from the natural rhythms and fibers of every day spiritual routines and images. These gave rise to a guiding narrative, formed from family practices, spiritual imagery, and activities that communicate a family's engagement with God's Word. In kitchen table youth ministry this narrative of natural rhythms functions as a supporting environment for families and church to share and enact the narratives of Scripture. This discussion of natural rhythms is in response to the high degree of professionalization in U.S. mainline Protestant churches — a trend that sadly contributes to the gap between parents' involvement with their children's faith formation and the church. This gap manifests itself mainly through the tendencies of families to outsource faith formation into the hands of Christian educators and youth ministers, unintentionally degrading the church's role in faith formation to mere babysitting or entertainment paradigms.

Kitchen Table Fellowship

Another powerful image around which I build the organizing themes of this book is that of table talk. My aunt and her family would host us around a large oak table, occasionally inviting the local minister. As a child and later as a youth, I would listen to the table talk of the adults, who discussed a variety of topics and never failed to discuss the church and theological issues. Table talk always sparked my curiosity about life, about God, and about the human situation. What confirmation instruction did not quite do for me, my family's stories about life did. Since my family belongs to the World War II generation, looking for God amid the tragedies of war put a human face on the heavily intellectual side of the Lutheran tradition. I memorized the confessional aspect of it and stayed unmoved till my propensity for existential thought had been stirred up by these real stories, still echoing pain and quest for God.

Kitchen table youth ministry resonates many of these themes, such as stirring the faith formation of children and youth by curiosity rather than dogma, using real-life stories as vehicles for introducing the complexity of human life, and bringing Scripture into dialogue with human questions, doubts, affirmations, and need for direction and security.

Space

I did not personally have a community of support grounded in my congregation, and I felt sort of spiritually afloat there. In contrast to this ecclesiastical lightness, I found gravity around the table, and this physical space mediated the abstract faith through its concreteness, reliability, and presence of human agents. In the postmodern world dominated by spiritual, family, or virtual flippancy, the question of space and moorings becomes quite pertinent. Given convoluted family reconfigurations, an ethereal virtual world, and the compromise of justice and democracy in a world of terror and economic globalization, what, I wonder, will ground youth's sense of direction, values, beliefs, and ethical response?

The Question of Grounding

The question of grounding is both physical (concerning its spatial dimension), and theological-epistemological (concerning the source of grounding and the ways to achieve it). In this book I propose to talk about the physicality and theology of grounding in terms of kitchen table fellowship. Kitchen table fellowship, like the kitchen table itself, I suggest, is balanced on four "legs": Gathering, Integration, Formation and Transformation, and Tradition. *Gathering* calls for the creation of a central space and a central activity that will foster human interaction and fellowship. I propose that it be a kitchen space and that the activity be the practice of table fellowship around the kitchen table. *Integration* emphasizes diversity around the kitchen table. This means that the kind of ministry that is practiced in the spirit of the kitchen table extends an invitation to all generations, to all people of different cultural, ethnic, racial, and socioeconomic backgrounds. This ministry involves the ways to practice meeting the stranger, intergenerational activities, and rhetorical strategies that are gender and difference inclusive, and generative. *Formation and transformation* employs the format of a story and storytelling when inviting the living Word of God to guide and shape our personal stories and the ways in which we experience and testify to God's presence in our lives. *Tradition* seeks to endow kitchen table youth ministry with the astuteness that the Christian church offers through its various forms of catechesis. The guiding question — "To what end are we forming our children and youth?" — can be answered only by drawing on the well of the centuries of Christian wisdom and experience that have nurtured the believers in faith.

I articulate the theological basis for the kitchen table fellowship by exploring the connection modeled by the Eucharistic fellowship. When the community of the faithful gathers around the sacrament, it experiences God's incarnational presence through the body and blood of Jesus Christ and the Word. The mystery of God's nearness is in its actuality manifested in very earthly fashion: through bread and wine (the products of soil), through the Word (the living active presence of Christ in the Holy Spirit manifested, for example, in the motions of one's heart), and through human agents (such as minister and the community of the believers) who proclaim the Word, remember it through the stories, and live it out through practices. This "earthiness" of God's presence in the sacrament of the Eucharist does not demystify or simplify the act of incarnation; rather, it suggests a possibility for a catechetical practice in which formation and transformation in the Word is experienced and reenacted in an earthly or embodied way (or kitchen table fellowship).

The ministry of the kitchen table also builds upon the interactive nature of God's Word, which inspires the imaginative construal of the Christian identity of all who dialogue with the Word and life itself. As families form youth in faith, their goal is to nurture youth in creating a faith-based narrative identity. In other words, spiritual formation unfolds itself as an interplay between the transformative power of the Word and a person's imagination, which allows for one's narrative of life to be rewritten by divine script. The Word of God rewrites human texts by disrupting and confronting the patterns of thought that fill in socially acceptable narratives. For example, the narratives of success, fashionable clothes, virtual profiles, physical beauty, etc., are offered to adolescents by culture as false (yet for many teenagers

real) narratives of friendship, values, or accomplishments. Therefore, forming youth in faith requires that parents, adult mentors,
and the church community as a whole coach youth in developing
narratives that are filled with stories of friendship, acting, and
speaking that are inspired by the Word of God in Scripture and
worship.

Who Is the Family?

In this book I use the term "family" in a rather generalized sense. I
am aware of the growing multicultural and pluralistic paradigms
that define the contemporary understanding of American family.
I am equally aware of the fragmentation and the woundedness
of family. In my own family there were three teenagers who were
growing up with a stepmother only a few years older than they.
She brought to the marriage and our household a young daughter
who called the teenagers' father by his first name. At my workplace I know of a young family who are raising their own child
along with a teenage daughter from the husband's previous marriage. This teenage daughter goes back and forth between her
father and her mother, who now lives with a boyfriend. I know
a student who is going through a divorce, who suddenly finds
himself having to fight over the shared custody of his two young
children. Not being able to wake up with them every morning
and say goodnight to them are among the hardest outcomes of
the divorce for this student.

I know at least two female students whose children live with
their husbands while they stay on campus during the week and
try to complete their seminary education. I know several homo-
sexual men who have formed families with their partners and
raise children together. In my homeland, Slovakia, couples tend
to get married when their children are well beyond first-grade age.
With these trends that have altered traditional family structures,
"family" in my proposed kitchen table youth ministry paradigm
refers to a presence of biologically related or unrelated adults who

can model nurture. Since sharing a meal is such a basic human need, I argue that it can take on the role of a practice that binds members of a biological or church family with a significant degree of intimacy and cohesion.

There are families who might be able to practice kitchen table ministry well if they are intentional about its practices; and there are families who might not be able to practice it because they are sole providers (single-parent families) who take on two or more jobs in order to put food on the table. If there is rarely an adult who can be present to a particular youth during dinnertime, I call on congregations to step in and fill this void. For although kitchen table youth ministry rests primarily on the shoulders of family, the congregations play a vital supporting role. In fact, I envision this as a simultaneous ministry in which families enforce and reenact the communal aspect of the Christian faith in their family milieu. Families who are unchurched or who are only beginning to form their relationship to a faith community can also practice kitchen table ministry. The starting point of this ministry is life stories rather than dogmas. However, this ministry develops its substantive nature by entering into a conversation with the Word of Scripture. Everyday stories can present the moral complexities of human life, but they need an interpretative framework able to substantiate the human quest for truth through a relationship with the divine. Kitchen table youth ministry presents this relationship as the family's engagement with the Word of God. The crux of this engaging relationship is its embodiment in human agents, space, and practices. Both churched and unchurched families need a supportive environment that can deepen their engagement with God's Word, and for this the ecclesial community is indispensable.

Methodology

Kitchen table youth ministry unfolds as an ongoing conversation between the history and tradition of the Christian church and the particular contemporary context in which the ecclesial practice is located. (In this book ecclesiastical practice refers to the practice of instructing and forming youth in the Christian tradition.) This conversation is facilitated by a confessional-correlational method of practical theology. The confessional aspect of the method stresses the transformative work of the Word as embodied in the Christian narrative. The Christian story, with its narrative and liturgical representations, is what shapes, educates, and guides the families and communities of faith on their faith journey. The correlational aspect of the method stresses the relationship between the Word of God and the sociocultural situatedness of an ecclesiastical practice. In its freedom the Word of God binds itself to a particular historical and social context of the church and the individual. By examining these contemporary contexts (family, economy, and cultural trends such as the use of technology, kitchen designs, eating and communication patterns in families, etc.), the correlational aspect seeks to come up with a relevant and authentic practice for engaging God's Word and the particularity of the human situation. In practical terms it means asking the question: In the twenty-first century what are the models of catechesis through which we can communicate faith effectively and confidently to children and youth? In order to answer this question, the correlational aspect of my method also emphasizes the Word as the active living presence of Christ, who binds himself freely not only to particular contexts, but also to human agents who mediate the nearness and transformative effect of God's Word. In the Word, God in Jesus Christ encounters a person and radically reshapes the ground of this person's existence. It is in the Word that God in Christ befriends sinful humanity and empowers us to form relationships with one another.

The families and communities that engage in kitchen table fellowship are inviting the living Word of God to guide their conversation and mediate the transformation of their human nature under the agency of the Word. They pledge to be there to assist young people in understanding and interpreting the truth of God's

Word. Kitchen table youth ministry accentuates the fact that if we want our youth to know, to experience, and to understand what relationship with God in Christ means, we need to offer our presence and commitment to them. Kitchen tables are there to make families and communities pause and capture special moments for God's Word in the web of relationships and fellowship.

Chapter One

Spiritual Formation at the Center of the Kitchen

WHEN I VISIT MY FAMILY in Slovakia, I try to catch up on the lives of my nephew and niece as best I can. Conversation with my eleven-year-old niece, Daniela, is about her rabbit, clothes, entertainment choices, girlfriend choices (blushing, rolling eyes, and pretended uninterest are still the response to questions about boyfriends), books and magazines, and lastly school. Conversation with my fifteen-year-old nephew, Martin, is something else. It usually goes like this:

> *Me:* How are you doing?
> *Martin:* Good.
> *Me:* How is school?
> *Martin:* Good.
> *Me:* Do your teachers give you lots of homework?
> *Martin:* Not bad.
> *Me:* What is your favorite subject?
> *Martin:* None.

(Martin is a straight A student and would like to be a science researcher.)

> *Me:* Were you able to make new friends?

(Martin has just moved to a new town and new school.)

> *Martin:* Yes.
> *Me:* What are their names?

Reluctantly Martin throws at me two or three names. During our conversation Martin usually texts or plays on his cell phone, and when I ask him if he is able to pay attention both to that and to *me*, he assures me that he can. Discouraged, I ask my mom (his grandmother) whether she gets the same kind of response. Mom nods, but also reveals her strategy: "When he answers me in his typical yes-no-good-don't know fashion, I tell him that that's not good enough for me. I tell him that I need to hear from and learn about him more," says Mom. To my question of whether she gets more out of him this way, she says that she does.

Youth and the Living Relationship with God in Christ: Looking for an Entry Point

Such frustrations and such tactics are not unfamiliar to us in seminary or church teaching situations, are they? A teaching colleague shared with the class that the most frequent type of a phone call she receives from the parents or youth ministers is one that asks for the best — meaning the most efficient, effective, and successful — curriculum for youth. The questions of how to nurture our children and youth in faith tend to be reduced to a frantic search for a miraculous curriculum. We think of it almost like prepackaged, quickly microwaveable nutrition through which we can feed faith, spirituality, and values to our offspring. Since it takes time and energy to bring up a child, curriculum seems to cater to the needs of time- and energy-depleted parents, teachers, and church professionals. Given my typical conversations with Martin — which always prove to be hard work for me — I too might be tempted to hope some curriculum will do what I cannot because I don't feel up to the hard work of engaging him or any youth in the questions of faith and God.

When I talk about engaging youth in the matters of faith, I mean not so much church attendance or participation in a youth group but nurturing knowledge — knowledge of self, the world, and God that anticipates rationally, experientially, emotionally, and intuitively God's presence in all spheres of human life and the universe. It is the knowledge of assurance that God in Christ is intimately and uniquely present in one's life. So how do I get started on this task? Where is my entry point for leading a youth into an assured and living relationship with God in Christ? My nephew Martin has been baptized and confirmed, attends church, and reads the Bible. At the same time, since his father's recent and tragic death, Martin has been quiet about his struggling faith. I sense that he has questions for God with regard to his father's death. I know that attending the church does not answer his questions or take away his struggles entirely. And so there he is — sitting in the pew with his faith that seeks to understand.

Martin is a prototype of a boy who has been churched since his birth. He has an experiential framework for his faith (through worship and liturgy), for its ritualistic progression (through baptism and confirmation), for faith rituals as practiced in our family (Christmas, Easter, All Souls' Day), and he has a developing cognitive framework for the contents of faith. The world of church is familiar to him and to his sister. When children grow up in families that share a Christian faith heritage, profess their commitment to it, and create the opportunities for their members to experience and learn about faith, spiritual formation becomes an organic ingredient of family life. It feels naturally aligned with the family's values and their world outlook. The question of an entry point still remains a valid question, yet the full force of this question becomes particularly potent in contexts where experiential understanding of faith is lacking. Such contexts include unchurched families, interreligious families, and fractured families who are unable to provide their children an overarching support and commitment to their spiritual growth. Both types of families — committed and churched families on the one hand and families who struggle with their dedication and belonging to a particular community of faith on the other — are faced with challenges regarding spiritual formation of their children and youth.

In the first situation, spiritual formation that feels like a natural part of a family's life can become merely a predictable routine. It can focus on reinforcing or entrenching children in the traditional ways that family thinks about and practices their faith. Children might be expected to follow the spiritual paths of their ancestors or display the same values. Their spiritual formation builds upon their familiarity with the Christian tradition and is expected to take a turn that will conform to the family's values. No doubt children's and youth's familiarity with the content and language of faith, its liturgical manifestations, and their experiences of faith helps adults with further nurturing the young in their faith. In the second situation, spiritual formation begins with an opportunity to introduce children and youth to a glimpse of the living promise of God in Christ. Without language, images, or experiences of faith, the adults cannot rely on children's or youth's "familiarity concept." The children's and youth's lack of familiarity with tradition can lead to adults' discomfort with how to engage them.

In both instances, spiritual formation begins with building a relationship with youth. The reason why curricula do not succeed in the longer run, even with the best intentions, is because they do not fully embody the reality of adult-youth relationship and friendship. When we contain children's and youth's minds through curricula and their ready-to-eat answers, we tend to indoctrinate rather than befriend. We tend to recycle tradition, but absent relationships, we do not really engage it. That is to say, engaging youth in the faith tradition calls for a reversal of steps: Confirmation preparation or any catechetical instruction does better if it follows (or at least engages simultaneously) a youth's curiosity about faith and God. We pass on faith by allowing it to be poked by the imagination, questions, and answers of children and youth themselves.

Curiosity about life, mystery, and the divine is an innate capacity of every person. This capacity is heightened with youth as they enter the stage of abstract thinking.[1] Abstract thinking (or formal operational thought) positions youth as seekers. Youth seek to understand: understand the world of life and tragedy, the world of love and pain, the world of adults, the world of God, and *their* own world. Minds and bodies that expand with overwhelming velocity desperately try to search for tools that will guide them through life's complexities and reveal to them the truth about themselves. James Fowler states that "the adolescent's religious hunger is for God who knows, accepts, and confirms the self deeply, and who serves as an infinite guarantor of the self with its forming myth of personal identity and faith."[2] What youth want from God is no different from what youth want from adults. (The difference is that only God in Christ is able to authenticate a person's worth and seal his or her image after the likeness of Christ.) Youth want and need adult guarantors in order to grow into self-assured sons and daughters, believers, and citizens in their local, global, and faith communities. Christian educator Kenda Dean says, "The most significant curriculum for any adolescent is the *person who teaches*.... For teenagers, revelation takes human form — which does not minimize the importance of doctrine, but explains why doctrine conveyed in the absence of trustworthy love falls on deaf ears."[3] Spiritual formation is fundamentally predicated upon embodying Christ's living presence as friendship: as commitment to values of trust, care, and above all love for children and youth.

Spiritual Formation and Survival

In her classic book about adolescent culture, Patricia Hersch began to address a phenomenon that since the publication of the book has been researched and written about by other scholars in the fields of youth ministry, education, and psychology.[4] This phenomenon reveals an unsettling truth, not so much about adolescents as about adults. Hersch calls her narrative *A Tribe Apart.*[5] The stereotypical adult interprets this title to mean it is the adolescents who pull away from us adults. Hersch documents that in actuality it is *we* who pull away from our adolescents. This gradual drifting away of adults from children and youth is a complex occurrence and one we have come to deem culturally normative in how we nurture and care for our families.

It is beyond the scope of this chapter to engage in a thorough sociocultural and historical analysis of the centrifugal forces affecting parents and their children. The phenomenon of physical, emotional, and spiritual separation of children and their parents has been gradually evolving in the milieu of our cultural and economic changes. This cultural and economic evolution has affected the structure of fairly stable institutions such as family, religion, the market economy, and the nation-state. In a Darwinian sense, the concept of evolution refers to a genetic flexibility of species by which they adjust to environmental fluctuations. The engine that sets into motion the variety of evolutionary processes is the instinct for survival. Evolutionary changes fuel human anxiety over survival; yet at the same time, they are the means to achieve survival. Evolution thus acts both as a means of expressing humanity's instinctual drive (to survive) and as an instrument to satisfy the drive.

However, if humankind focuses more on instrumentality in the evolutionary process rather than its telos (i.e., what is the end-goal of our survival), then survival becomes a mindset of competition. Some of my former parishioners who lived through the Cold War era built a bunker in their backyard, filling it up with everything from food to blankets and pillows. When they showed it to me, it was clear that they were proud of their ability to plan survival after an atomic bomb. Is the end-goal of our survival acquisition, accumulation, and collection of material possessions? Is the end-goal of our survival passing on our genetic capital? Or is it shaping a community that will put forth a vision for the future in which our values, habits, and culture will be preserved and honored, yet in a visionary way adjusted to a new social matrix? If a society does not frame its instinctual need to survive within a philosophical and theological framework, it will reduce survival from a noble sharing of communal wisdom and resources to a cutthroat game of competition. Survival based on competition becomes a disembodied, isolated race dominated by evolutionary forces of nature, economy, and religion, in which the individual forsakes loyalty to community and humanity. When we lose our commitment to a question of "to what end do we survive," we lose our understanding for the common human predicament.

Cultural and Economic Evolution

Discussion about the end-goal of survival in contemporary U.S. society is guided by various ideologies, such as consumerism, a populist extension of the Cold War ideology that divides the world rather simplistically into good and bad nations, individualistic pursuits of happiness and personal salvation, etc. What are the recent cultural and economic manifestations of evolutionary changes? On a cultural level, transitioning from modernity to postmodernity has shaken the ground of foundational beliefs, values, and traditional structures (such as nuclear family) to the point of creating anxiety in society. In his insightful book on postmodern spirituality, Barry Taylor talks about the resurgence of the Gothic.[6] The Gothic functions as a cultural channel through which people express their fears and feelings of insecurity that accompany the loss of a solid world and the arrival of an elusive one, like postmodernity. The gothic focus on the shadowy side of life taps into people's lack of trust in the science and rationalism of modernity. In postmodernity, the dictates of science are replaced with society's uncertainty about how to protect life, health, the environment, and shelter itself against the forces of evil. The liquification of a once solid world, dominated by universally agreed upon categories and values, requires a new set of skills. Taylor argues that just as digging in a world that is completely liquid is no longer a useful skill, so too is trying to adhere to the old, customary ways of thinking and practicing faith. The new skill, as he suggests, is that people explore surfaces and the width of knowledge instead of exploring depth.[7] Communication scholars call the new trend informationism and the skill high-tech literacy. This skill gets people entangled in a broad web of cultural and economic influences, stimuli, and previously unconceived expressions of their values. People are being challenged to imagine themselves in the realm of new personal, family, and social reconfigurations. A good example of my point is the reinvention of family.

Traditional definitions of family as a nuclear unit that is comprised of father, mother, and children have been redefined by a new sociological reality in which children are raised through a diversity of family models. Don Browning talks about the diversity of family models in U.S. society today in terms of a new pluralism — a pluralism that includes single-parent families, families with a stepparent or same-sex parents, and cohabitating families.[8] This pluralism finds its expression also in the spheres of economy and household. Our service economy has us deal with customer service located in India. A TV commercial shows a mother who conducts a meeting with her company via her laptop: half of her body dressed in a suit, the other half in pajamas and slippers. Next to her sits an infant whom she also manages to feed while giving her online presentation. Pluralism of lifestyles goes much further than fashion styles. It blurs the boundaries between domestic and work places, between duty to work and duty to nurture or between a company's commitment to local communities vis-à-vis market incentives abroad.

Informationism takes away existential anxiety over the future by making culture turn to the present. With the past distant and the future opaque, the moment becomes the chic paradigm onto which society holds for its self-definition and security. Immersion in high-tech environments becomes a culturally expressed mode of indwelling the moment in the contemporary U.S. society. People survive by seizing the immediacy of their lives. Survival becomes a way of life in which a person interacts with surfaces (gathering information). We grow in our knowledge of life by gathering data *about* life. This is at the expense of accruing knowledge *of* life through wisdom, a process that occurs when we engage life as a source of constantly changing love and pain, growth and diminishment. When we refuse to live our lives through the pain of our tragedies and through the joy of our victories, but instead interact with it in a disengaged way, we become well-versed *about* ourselves but not well-versed in the intimate knowledge *of* ourselves. To live one's life in the way of informationism is to describe it instead of owning it. Quentin Schultze argues that informationism thrives on desubjectifying human relationships to the degree of securing them as the smooth flow of information that will benefit an individual's self-interests.[9] Through the lens of informationism, "We imagine cultures not as organic ways of life but as computer-like networks — closed systems that persons can objectively observe, measure, manipulate, and eventually control."[10] The age of high technology offers a means to personal survival through which an individual accumulates data and property and gets a false sense of personal empowerment by seizing control of other human beings (who are viewed as competitors in the survival game of life).

On an economic level, the work and the economy exert enormous pressures upon contemporary families. The number of women who joined the work force almost doubled between 1960 and 2006, with both men and women spending around 62.8 hours per week at work.[11] Families are stressed by the task of providing for their members, and given the lack of safety nets that are in place with more socialist governments, their failure to provide can have hard results. A decentralized market economy can provide healthy competition as well as give rise to high levels of anxiety. "Financial anxiety," says Robert Putnam, "is associated ... with less frequent moviegoing ... less time spent with friends, less card playing, less home entertaining, less frequent attendance at church, less volunteering, and less interest in politics."[12] Reinventing and adapting to constantly changing models of family, work economy, and home economy become significant survival skills. As a culture that constructs its identity in survival, we generate and reward anxiety at the same time. We exalt the intensity of production and workaholism into virtue. Anxious to survive, we produce more and are rewarded for it. When anxiety fuels our need for self-worth and self-authentication, it transforms itself from being a necessity for survival to being a permanent and culturally agreed-upon *modus vivendi*. Obsession with material possessions, consumption, and ownership "becomes more than acquiring what one needs for material survival; it moves into the realm of meaning making."[13] With regard to family, adopting anxiety as the ground of our purpose and being gives birth to values that Don Browning identifies as "increasing individualism, growing preoccupation with individual fulfillment, wider tolerance for divorce."[14]

Survival is an instinct. As human beings we have allowed instinct to fuel our moral imagination when it comes to articulating grounds for virtuous living. Survival cradles our cultural virtues (such as informationism) and economic virtues (such as workaholism). In other words, survival as an instinct becomes a highly individualized enterprise, diminishing values of the communal body such as kinship, altruism, and caring. Noble survival is a highly communal enterprise, balancing the values of individual self such as individual rights, property, and freedom. According to sociobiologists, survival in nature does not build upon the individualized, but rather upon a group telos.[15] If nature can survive only collectively, why does the human race want to do it on its own?

When Survival Is Nurture

What happens when survival becomes a paradigm for passing on faith to our children and youth? In trying to survive, adults abandon their young. The forms of abandonment can be physical such as with Nebraska's new "safe haven" law that allows parents or caretakers to surrender their children even beyond their infancy without recrimination.[16] Emotional or spiritual abandonment implies the loss of intentionality in providing nurture to children and youth. The loss of the ability to nurture in meaningful ways occurs because "for today's parents, childrearing may often be in conflict with career, with finding a new mate, with loyalties to children from previous marriages, and with retaining even a modest standard of living."[17] Changes from the industrial era into the postindustrial era, from manufacturing to service economies facilitate the views of care and nurture as services to be handed over to others. Formation in the hands of professionals seeps in as an inevitable direction for raising one's children. From an early age children shuttle back and forth between parents and babysitters, sports coaches, school teachers, Sunday school teachers, piano teachers, ballet teachers, tutors, etc. Errand specialists administer their medications, fix their meals, and drive them around. Many times there is no one for the children and youth to bounce back to in between times. The shift in values (including the value of what constitutes family nurture) has produced new cultural norms. Chap Clark writes, "We have evolved to the point where we believe driving is support, being active is love, and providing any and every opportunity is selfless nurture. We are a culture that has forgotten how to *be* together."[18]

Kitchen Table Youth Ministry: Intentionality of Home, Time, and Space

I believe that most families genuinely wish to do their best at nurturing their children in faith. Elizabeth F. Caldwell writes: "In listening to the concerns and questions of parents, I hear confessions of inadequacy, requests for answers to specific questions asked by a child, and sincere requests for help: How do I begin to talk about faith with my child?"[19] It appears to me that these questions, although important, are not the fundamental questions with which to begin the Christian nurture of children. Instead, I propose a kind of nurture that asks probing questions about the quality of one's relationship with one's children and youth. I propose starting spiritual formation with questions such as these: Do we have a home or a house? Do we eat meals together, and if so, how, when, and when not? Where do we eat? And how often do we do so (alone or together)? How often do we typically spend time talking together, and when and where?

To predicate spiritual formation on the categories of home, time, and space counteracts the loneliness that is a by-product of a society that exalts work above all else. Sharon D. Parks writes, "In the domain of economic life, we typically remain strangers to one another — each of us essentially alone with our sense of busyness and cumber, fear and guilt."[20] Nurture in faith takes a form of what feminist and womanist scholars call the art of homemaking or homesteading. It means the art of cultivating with children and youth the sense of sharing in humanity, rootedness in family and faith values, vocational empowerment, and imaginative participation in the world. It also means creating a site of resistance. Womanist author bell hooks talks about homeplace as a place where traditionally African Americans "could freely confront the issue of humanization."[21] Contemporary families live in a culture that finds ways to dehumanize and alienate them from the true source of authenticity and affirmation, that is, God in Christ. From consumerism and media propaganda to politicized church gospels and nationalist ideologies such as real patriotism, real believ-ism, and real American-ism, families' efforts to achieve integrity in the meaning-making process are sabotaged by these competing and polarizing ways of finding an authentic self. Effects on the young and the vulnerable members of the family are even greater.

In order to instill an integral sense of value making, families need to practice homemaking. bell hooks talks about homeplace as a place of resistance. Traditionally African Americans used it to resist oppressive and dehumanizing practices of white supremacy. The struggle for liberation is not over for contemporary families either. "Oppressed" by workaholism, consumption, and xenophobia, families do well to focus on homesteading as a place, vision, and practice of enabling, empowerment, and emancipation of mind, body, and soul. "Homemaking and homesteading are activities which build a space where souls can thrive and dream — secure, protected, related, nourished, and whole."[22] Homemaking requires intentionality, not only of hearing the voice of the young and being the voice to them, but intentionality of having a space, creating practices of homemaking, and allocating time for them.

Eucharist at Home

My model of kitchen table youth ministry situates homemaking in a theological ground. Homemaking as a ministry of nurture in God's Word requires the tangible presence of people who gather together around a meal, share and celebrate the Word, and send forth people from the community and receive them back into the community. The cyclical notion of nurture structured around a meal, a story, and communal empowerment is grounded in the Eucharistic feast. The sacrament of the Eucharist embodies the reality of divine hospitality and nourishment. Its elements (bread and wine) tell the story of Christ's crucifixion and our reconciliation with God through Christ. The Eucharist sustains our spiritual strength and fervor to carry out the Word and calls us back to a continual remembrance and celebration of our relationship with the Trinitarian God. In the Eucharist God reveals God-self both through Christ's enfleshedness (body and blood) and through the Word in Christ (proclamation). At the table we continue to embody Christ's flesh by demonstrating the reality of God's self-revelation as a human with tangibles (physical presence, words of care, feeding, etc.) Simultaneously, at the table we have the opportunity to proclaim or share the Word of Scripture and recreate the incarnational presence of God.

Central to my notion of kitchen table youth ministry is of course the metaphor of a kitchen table. Both as a concrete piece of furniture and as a metaphorical representation of the Eucharistic table, the kitchen table symbolizes our response to our profound human yearning for belonging and togetherness. It taps into a person's ontological anxiety at being separated from the ground of God's being. Only in community can individuals restore the grounds of their existence — that is, being one with and in communion with God in Christ. The painful feeling of alienation can be healed and transformed only in an embodied way: by putting flesh on God's promises of love, trust, forgiveness, and communion. As Jesus Christ fulfilled God's promises through his own flesh, corporeality of love becomes a means through which to nurture human relationships into intimacy and unity with God.

The kitchen table grounds people in the reality of communion and intimate relationships by creating the opportunity for table fellowship. Table fellowship means inviting people to share both the human presence and the presence of God with one another and to cultivate the values of friendship, membership, solidarity, and tolerance. A family practices table fellowship when it intentionally generates activities that will promote trust, a sense of belonging, and bonding among its members. These activities typically include sharing meals together, welcoming others at the table, conversation and storytelling, reading, playing games together. Such table fellowship is a counterpoint to our dominant mode of being. For typically when our youth cry out, "Will you be there for me?" families and institutions respond by loading youth with more busyness. More programming from the churches, more extracurricular activities from the parents, and more homework from the schools are the responses by which we as a society tend to answer the lonely cries of our youth.

Outsourcing Homemaking

Intentionality in creating space, time, and practice for the spiritual nurture of children and youth is hard to achieve with a lifestyle that is fast paced, tightly scheduled, and work-obsessed. The outcome of such schedules is latchkey children — children who eat alone, dream alone, and do homework alone. The working demands upon U.S. families have significantly altered the nature of home. The virtues of homemaking (and by that I mean the activities and practices that bind the family members) have been outsourced into the hands of paid professionals who run people's households and raise their children. Maggie Jackson, in her book *What's Happening to Home?* documents a widespread transformation (or mutation?) of home into a hotel.[23] The basic household activities that used to bind the members of the family into a unit, such as preparing the meals, grocery shopping, cleaning house, lawn-mowing, or decorating the Christmas tree have been transformed into tasks that a family no longer claims as theirs, but instead views as specialized and paid tasks to be performed by outsiders (cooks, errand specialists, cleaners, lawn care professionals).[24]

Jackson raises a question of what distinguishes a home from a hotel when we have a maid, a chef, a babysitter, a maintenance person, a personal secretary, an errand specialist. Now of course not every household can afford all these professionals, but many do choose to afford some. Yet the question I want to raise is not that of social class. It is the question of family ecology that has been seriously disrupted by putting parents' needs above their children's. David Elkind writes, "For the middle-income child today, it is hard to see the necessity of being relegated to a baby sitter or sent to a nursery school or day care center when he or she has a perfectly nice playroom and yard at home.... It seems so unnecessary, so clearly a reflection of parent and not child need."[25]

Typically, people who hire professionals to do all or some of their household and parenting tasks do so because they do not have time or energy to do it themselves. The Pew Internet and American Life Project documents the falling number of hours that mothers are able to devote to household chores because of the intensity of their paid work.[26] Exhausted from the workday, parents opt for letting strangers into their personal space. The perception of what is real in the family fades away with every step toward professionalization of household duties. Jackson writes, "Each time we cook, clean, or mend, we're creating opportunities for talking, for being together with those who share our home. We are creating the glue that binds us to the humans we love."[27]

I grew up in a tiny two-bedroom communist-style apartment. I had to fight with my brother over working space or space on the sofa to watch TV. The kitchen table was too small for us to be able to spread our elbows comfortably, and the bathroom could hardly accommodate one person. In that space, elbows and bodies were tangible, noises too close to one's ear, smells too sharp to ignore. Family was *real*. At that time I wished for the kind of spacious house with a private bathroom that I sporadically saw in movies from the West. Now I have that. But because of geographical distance and health concerns, neither my family nor my husband's family can visit and stay with us any longer. Comparing the abode of my childhood with the abode of my adulthood, I come closer to describing the absence of home: home that is empty of or lacking in the presence of people, voices, smells, fights, laughter, conversations, or work, is void of its fundamental content and quality — that is, void of community and humanity.

Kitchen Table or Island:
Where Do Families Eat and Talk?

Kitchen table youth ministry offers a way for cultures, communities of faith, and families to *share* this togetherness I knew as a child and now miss as an adult living an ocean away from my family. Since people's sense of community in the twenty-first century is built upon virtual markers of human companionship, such as cell phones, e-mail, chat rooms, and TVs, a kitchen space proves to be a viable alternative to a virtual habitat. According to kitchen designer Terence Conran, it is the kitchen space that appeals to people who want to be together. He says, "[Kitchen] can offer a means of grounding yourself in reality, a touchstone of tastes, smells, and texture."[28] In her book on kitchen designs, Susan Maney Lovett also raises the importance of kitchens, saying: "This one room has become so important, in fact, that prospective buyers consider it a primary factor in selecting a home."[29] Remodeling experts note the same trend. Tom Troland, senior market analyst from Meredith Research Solutions, says this: "Without question, the kingpin of consumer home remodels is the kitchen. It consumes more attention, energy, finances, and complex decision-making than any other project, short of building an entirely new house."[30] The home remodeling boom seems to attest to families' desire to create a convivial ambiance for their members.[31] For example, in 2008 the winner of the design competition organized by the National Kitchen and Bath Association is an integrative model of the kitchen. According to a design plan description, the goal of the kitchen remodeling project was to connect inside and outside environments (such as pool or garden). In this project the kitchen has become the central piece of the house, securing the connectedness of the space.[32]

On one hand, the remodeling emphasis on kitchens is an emphasis upon securing a sense of community.[33] The creation of an open floor plan that dominates current home designs has the kitchen becoming a multipurpose space, sometimes called a great room. Taking on the functions of the kitchen, living, and dining rooms all at the same time, the great room offers a space in which the members of a family can interact with one another. According to Susan Maney Lovett, kitchens no longer represent sequestered areas for cooking, but rather cater to people's hobbies, working demands, and interests.[34] In order to accommodate the idea of family space, kitchens have become larger. With increasing human traffic in the kitchens, designers are concerned with making the space manageable for kitchen tasks.

Thus islands or peninsulas are inserted to organize the kitchen work triangle. In designer's terminology, the work triangle refers to the space between the range, refrigerator, and sink. The islands can have built-in sinks, cooktops, storage shelves, or pot racks suspended above them. They help to keep the triangle sides short and accessible.[35] They can be built-in or movable. They can have raised countertops to accommodate chairs and offer a sit-down opportunity. Larger kitchens might have multiple triangles, with islands then duplicating the needed workstations as double-sink, cooktops, or shelving. The island is the center that enables a person to flow smoothly in the kitchen space.

The islands are popular and highly demanded. The main purpose of an island is to provide functionality and efficiency to kitchens. With kitchens as multipurpose rooms, the islands divide the open space between the food preparation area and living or entertaining room. Islands regulate not only the functionality of the workflow or space, but also that of relationships. Those who are not helping the cooks by their own volition or by the cook's volition find themselves on the other side of the island. The islands also aim at bringing families together. In kitchen designs, islands many times connect the stray corners into a central place where a family can gather.

The idea of the kitchen as a multipurpose room is not the innovative creation of modern home designers; rather, the idea draws on some traditional forms of living found in farming communities. At the heart of the farmhouse stands the kitchen, which both physically and symbolically united family in its work and leisure. Architect Christopher Alexander describes life in the farmhouse in the following way: "The family activity centered around a big table in the middle: here they ate, talked, played cards, and did work of all kinds including some of the food preparation."[36] The common room was a gathering place for all the generations — grandparents, parents, and children — and provided the venue for family stories, busyness, and rest. Structurally, the way in which families create their home layouts and remodel kitchens tries to meet their deeply felt need for community. The idea of a kitchen as an open space reflects a desire for unobstructed flow of people, energy, and activities. But what about the practice of sharing the space and each other's presence? Are families committed to sharing the common, open space, and do they do it?

Kitchen Table: Sharing in Food, Sharing in Humanity, Sharing in Divine Care

Says Terence Conran, "The kitchen is one of the few remaining places where families can be guaranteed to spend at least some time together."[37] However, a kitchen space in itself does not suffice for bonding a family or a group of people into a unit. A center is needed. Traditionally, it has been the kitchen table that took on a centralizing role of family life. The concept of a kitchen table is invested with a deep symbolism. Theologian Letty Russell, in her discussion of feminist ecclesiology, employs the metaphor of a kitchen table to stress a close connection between kitchen tables and everyday human lives. Describing the context of East Harlem, she says: "The kitchen table is the scene of arguments, reprimands, and fighting as well as the scene of counting up the small cash supply or filling out forms for court or the welfare office. As the center of daily life it reflects the basic activities of the families, both good and bad."[38] Even the American media are catching up on the symbolism of the kitchen table in their discussion of everyday struggles of the American family. For example, the television network ABC has introduced a *Kitchen Table* series, inviting its viewers to talk about their struggles with paying the mortgage, saving for college tuition, affording elder care and health care, and other issues. The kitchen table talk metaphor likewise is beginning to find its place in the vocabulary of politicians who address the economic anxieties of the nation.

Communal eating or sharing of the meals is at the center of a family life and kitchen table fellowship. Across the fields of anthropology, theology, and architecture, there is a common agreement — as summarized by Christopher Alexander — that "communal eating plays a vital role in almost all human societies as a way of binding people together and increasing the extent to which they feel like 'members' of a group."[39] Food itself is indispensable in helping to bring people together in order to open their lives to one another. Terence Conran argues that "Good food, particularly good food eaten in company, promotes a deep sense of well-being."[40]

Around the table, the bonds of trust, belonging, and fellowship in the family are formed. Columbia University, home to leading researchers on the eating practices of the families in the United States, suggests that children and youth who eat dinners with their families on a regular basis are less likely to become involved in smoking, alcohol consumption, or taking drugs.[41] They perform better academically and have a greater sense of bonding with their families. The benefits of family suppers are reported also in relationship to treating eating disorders successfully.[42] However, the greatest benefit of having a family meal is the message it conveys: We have time for one another, and we care for one another. Having a meal together lays the groundwork for the experience of belonging. We belong to a family, community, and culture by virtue of specific dishes and ingredients, eating habits and table manners, practices of hospitality and table talk. We learn nonviolence by the way we hold the fork. We learn the boundaries, focus, and attention around the table based upon our sitting postures.[43] We learn to cohere as a group because through meals we attend to primordial human needs to feed and to be fed, to care and to be cared about. The commitment of adults to show care in this tangible way is to manifest to their children this sense of reliance on one another. Miriam Weinstein in her book *The Surprising Power of Family Meals* argues with regard to restaurant eating that "when we remove eating from the home, we weaken the bonds of affection and duty."[44]

Our kitchen designs might be conducive to family time, but our lifestyles are not. Destructuring family meals at the expense of structuring soccer or volleyball practices makes our duty to nurture and offer nourishment inferior to our duty to schedules and busyness. The primary practices of fellowship where sharing is practiced and internalized are replaced by the activities that promote both competition and teamwork, but in the spirit of "you need these activities in order to get into Ivy League schools." With their hectic life-styles people disturb the ecology of family eating. Fellowship over food as the primary practice of bonding and nurture has degenerated, as Michael Pollan suggests, from a cultural ritual to "a mechanical process of fueling the body."[45] He further explains that people no longer eat, but snack.[46] The times between meals lack structure or ritual; instead, the act of eating has been prolonged to a perpetual snacking at home, at work, and on the road. As Robert Putnam's research documents, restaurants, diners, and luncheonettes were replaced by fast-food chains that are mushrooming to feed lonely and hurried people.[47] More and more of the population eat alone, with family members eating at different times and in different places of the house (e.g., in front of the TV, at the computer desk, or sitting on one's bed). Families are also divided along dietary lines. What this means is that when a family sits down for a meal, the family members do it individually and with different types of food on their plates.[48]

Our youth are growing up without a sense of family rituals and family togetherness. The physical growth of children corresponds to the decline of family meals.[49] Yet fourteen-year-olds are too young to be left on their own, and the intentionality of the parents to stay in a relationship with their child needs to be more acute, not less.[50] Abandoning certain rituals such as communal meals, families give in to survival pressures. The paradigms of nurture are dictated by the values of competition, achievement, and success. The greatest challenge that youth face in today's society is to perform highly. Parents argue with their sons and daughters about "grades, future plans, and achievement in society, not about sexuality and not about values in general."[51] Empirical studies of the adolescent population suggest that young people perceive nurture and care that they receive from their families as a requirement to meet their parents' personal agendas, but not theirs.[52] If nurture becomes a subject of met and unmet demands, performances or requirements, the relationships it shapes will become conflictual and stressful. Chap and Dee Clark write that parents fear conflict and highly charged encounters with their teenage children.[53] If the pendulum swings too far in the direction of anxiety in a family, parents tend to choose a disengaged style of parenting, leaving children to their own devices.

Fear and survival force adults to create a matrix of social engagement in which the entry point into a relationship as well as managing that relationship is mediated by impersonal and professionalized ways of human interaction. From technology to professional staffs of teachers, coaches, therapists, youth ministers, or errand specialists, the families outsource nurture and care of their young. Formation and socialization become the concern of experts who conduct the discourse and guide the interactions. Or it becomes the matter of virtual forums that shape the interactions. The rules for personal engagements are formulated by impersonal agents and voices that are not steeped in a community or family.

Philosopher Paul Ricoeur writes that "there is no sociology of the neighbor. The science of the neighbor is thwarted by the praxis of the neighbor. One does not *have* a neighbor. I make myself someone's neighbor."[54] Similarly, we don't need a sociology of family only because our families are not comprised of sociological objects. What we desperately need is a praxis of family. A sociology of family facilitates establishing a functional kitchen design, but a praxis of family means creating family practices through which families mutually share in humanity and communality. Having a meal together *is* a practice of sharing. We literally share the resources such as food, space, time, and energy to prepare it, but we also share one another, and we share a pattern of divine care. As I was conversing with a children's minister from one of the Lutheran churches, she sighed about the children and youth who do not sit down for a family meal. "How will they understand the spiritual richness of the Eucharist if they do not have an experience of the table at home?" she asked.

At the family table we practice *ordo,* or the worship order. The tradition of *ordo,* as explained by Fred Edie, helps Christian believers to structure their lives into a living ecology of faith.[55] Edie's insight has important implications for constructing a praxis of nurture in the family. It charges families to re-create the sacramental and communal life of the church and then tie it to their individual lives. The blueprint of nurture then is embedded in the holy matrix of the church's sacramental life and life in the world. Life-giving sacraments and life-shaping practices order human lives into patterns of meanings, relating, doing, and being. Living an ecology of faith means that we do not allow these patterns of love, care, and reconciliatory relationships to be reconfigured or abandoned outside the worship service or church. In the world our lives represent holy patterns, forged by God's love and grace in Christ. By having a family meal, we carry the Eucharistic table into our households and nurture our children in the memory, experience, and image of divine care and love.

You can begin kitchen table youth ministry by:

♦ *Evaluating your kitchen space*

I encourage each family to pay attention to their kitchen design. Ask the following questions:

1. Does our kitchen space include a comfortable seating arrangement (not a sofa) where we can take time to eat and talk?

2. Do we have a table or an island at which to eat? Reflect on your eating experience when sitting at the table and at the island and focus on possible differences in the experiences.

3. What electronic media (such as TV or radio) might be intruding upon the sanctity of our family time?

◆ *Keeping a log of your family schedule*

I encourage each family to keep a log (start with a week and gradually extend this up to a month) of a daily schedule. Record the following data:

1. Dinner. Do we eat/not eat dinner?
2. Time of dinner. Is dinnertime the same every evening? Can and do all members of family come for dinner?
3. Regularity of dinner. How many times per week do we sit down for dinner?
4. Activities. Focus especially on activities that interfere with your dinnertime. Which of the activities can you reschedule or skip in order to be present at dinner? Which of them do you have to keep?

◆ *Making Connections*

I encourage each family to begin to make connections between divine care and family care when gathering for a meal. If you have a regular experience with the Eucharist, use your church experience to draw parallels between the spiritual care and nourishment of the Eucharist and your home table. Or you can use the experience of your home table fellowship to engage Scripture and look for passages in which themes of table fellowship, eating, hospitality, or feeding are narrated. What do you learn? This suggestion is appropriate for a congregational Bible study in that it focuses on helping families to see theological connections between sacramental and home life.

Chapter Two

Table Fellowship: Real or Virtual?

L ATELY MY PARENTS AND I have been talking about what to give my nephew and niece for Christmas. My mom suggested that I buy Daniela a small TV. I wondered aloud, Why? They have a TV. My parents explained that when the siblings watch TV together, they tend to get into fights over which show to watch. As the older sibling, Martin usually wins the fight and makes his sister yield to his preferences. "You cannot imagine," said my mom, "how much screaming and hurt feelings on Daniela's part this silly fighting generates. If she had a TV in her room, she could watch her favorite shows, and the house would be more peaceful." Mom also reminded me about the time in my teenage years when I wanted to watch a French romantic movie but was overruled by my father and brother who were set on watching World Cup Soccer. I can still vividly remember the disappointment of that moment. Being the youngest, I did not easily win family skirmishes over TV preferences. Yet, in retrospect, I am grateful that we had only one TV because it meant we had to watch it *together*.

Fragmentation of family cohesion does not occur only in the wake of traumatic events like a divorce or the death of a parent or a child. A family's unity and strength are also put to the test by the number of TV sets, computers, and other high-tech gadgets that silently prey on tenuous moments in family fellowship. As a family's high-tech inventory grows, so also do the minutes of diminished attention, lack of conversation, and loss of shared intimacy. Technology becomes our companion on our life journey. I travel extensively, and this is what I often see at airports: when people are not using their laptops, they squeeze them close to their bodies, holding them against their chests, almost as if hugging them. I wonder, is this body-laptop symbiosis an unconscious manifestation of our feelings of bonding and dependence upon our technology? A similar question can be asked regarding cell phones. What are we squeezing to our ears? Is it a cell phone or is it a "friend" that enables us to be connected with family and friends? Technology can represent the bridge to a human world of connectedness, family fellowship, or work and private relationships. Without that bridge, humans might very well feel lost in the habitat of human community that is their own yet in which they increasingly do not know how to navigate.

Spiritual Formation in the Hands of Technology: Preying on Three Longings of Youth

The formative power of technology lies in its lore of the egalitarian sharing of resources, knowledge, and relationships. In transposing the principles of the democratization of human discourse and resources into a virtual space, we witness both a release from geographical and sociocultural confinement and conformity to a particular way of being. On the one hand, creating a virtual space — a dimension of human existence that is free of institutional and communal authentication of values — is an effort to emancipate mind, body, and soul from modernity's ecclesial and family traditionalism, scientific rationalism, and economic conservatism. On the other hand, by forging a new space for emancipated existence that has peculiar organizing principles for human interaction and togetherness, we do not in fact entirely liberate ourselves. We fashion a supposedly free virtual human association but fall for its terms and contracts. In so doing, we allow virtual communities to shape our habits of thinking and being, thus growing into a different form of captivity. The appeal of virtual communities for youth is their promise to meet the following longings of youth: the need to belong, the need for freedom from tradition and conformity, and the need to find a place.

Michael Bugeja, a communication scholar, argues that humans desperately long for acceptance into community, and that increasingly people are finding such acceptance and welcome in cyberspace.[1] The hospitality of a virtual community may be a chimeric welcome, yet it is a welcome a thousand times better than that of an empty apartment or apathetic relationships. Youth in particular experience a keen desire for such acceptance and love. This longing for genuine intimacy and belonging develops in the context of youth's budding sexuality and intellectual capacity. During adolescence, youth experience a heightened awareness of their sexuality. They seek intimacy and love; they want to be known and accepted, and the body is essential to their efforts to be known. Through piercing, tattoos, sex, eating disorders, and self-mutilations, youth use their bodies in an effort to make themselves known to the outside world. Their physical appearance is likewise frequently used by youth to acquire love and intimacy. Christian educator James Loder observes that "intimacy and accurate love is a desperate need, [and one's] sexuality is a proximate and deficient longing for a deeper intimacy."[2] Youth take the physical realities of their bodies, space, or noise to seize the veracity of genuine love in human relationships, including those between youth and their parents, other adults, or peers. In their search for true love, adolescents actually feel lonely. The feeling of evasive love that is exacerbated by absent-minded relationships leads to pervasive feelings of loneliness, hopelessness, despair, and depression.[3]

On a cognitive level, youth begin to develop the formal operations of abstract thinking. This new mental faculty enables them to ponder theories and concepts and also to construct abstract theories on their own. The new faculty challenges youth to construct a meaningful ideology. Youth have an ideological hunger that makes them "uncompromisingly loyal to causes and... superb advocates and proselytizers."[4] Christian educator Kenda Dean sees the effects of this new skill in terms of young people's need for passion.⁵ Youth want to feel moved, excited, transported beyond their ordinary selves. Dean argues that if this developmental need is not adequately met by the church, young people are more likely to engage in, for example, sex, drugs, and high adrenalin sports. Youth can also surrender to apathy, lack of interest, boredom, and passivity. Youth are not cognitively or emotionally fully equipped for dealing with life's intricacies, for they lack life experience, and if they also lack adult guidance, they can easily slide into risky behavior, despair, and even suicide.⁶

Young people struggle with understanding their place in family or society through the process of individualization. "Individualization" refers to adolescence from a sociological perspective and includes renegotiating the social roles that adolescents hold. Christian educator Rick Osmer suggests three ways in which youth individualize: (1) by renegotiating their ties with and places in family when reaching economic independence, (2) by participating in society based upon their skills and knowledge, (3) by constructing their system of morality.⁷ Youth also struggle to establish an integral sense of self (or identity). This process is referred to as "individuation" and describes youth from a psychological perspective. In Eriksonian terms, individuation refers to the adolescent's process of identity formation. It is a process that oscillates between two poles: identity and role confusion. During this process an adolescent's fidelity to people, values, and personal identifications with role models from childhood is being reworked. This is a phase of experimentation in which adolescents sort through their childhood "treasures" that are used to determine their sexuality, viewpoints, roles, and loyalties to adults. Whether it is a song, a piece of clothing, a mom's prayer, a dad's *bon mot*, a grandpa's Bible, or a tree in which they used to hide with friends, these treasures no longer affirm the adolescent; on the contrary, they might feel alien and urgently need to be shaken off.

The existential upheaval of an adolescent's psyche manifests itself in doubting one's sexual identity and human worth, and in showing a tenuous commitment to work, love, or ideology. The healthy outcome of the process is when an adolescent achieves a consistent sense of self. After the process of exploration and evolving commitments to different systems of values of parents, friends, and culture, adolescents choose their own system of values, goals, and commitments. Their identity, says James Fowler, "communicates to others a sense of personal unity or integration."[8] Being accepted in a role and place that the adolescent fights hard to craft — in symbiosis with innate predispositions, intuitions, gifts, and callings — is what adolescents want from adults. Adolescents represent crafting-in-progress, and as much as they explicitly repudiate the imagery of parental art, implicitly they are also drawn to it. The images of parental art have lasting effects. However, during adolescence the art of parenting becomes the art of bricolage, and its effect is commingled with other influences. The influence of family is juxtaposed with the influences of technology, peers, consumerism, and the outward rejection of the adolescent's tribe. I turn first to the influence of technology.

Where All People Are Welcome: Democratization of Human Relationships in Cyberspace

An advocate of technology sees it as a forum for fostering democracy of human discourse and connectivity in human community. Robert Putnam states, "Research has shown that on-line discussions tend to be more frank and egalitarian than face-to-face meetings. They tend to ease users' anxiety about communicating across hierarchical, gender, or race boundaries."[9] With regard to family connectedness, Don Tapscott argues that technology can in fact be an ally to stressed and overwhelmed families. "The new media," he says "can certainly alleviate some of the disconnectedness of these children and families."[10] Tapscott's argument is consistent with the data provided by the Pew Internet and American Life Project research.[11] Families with children score highest in their ownership of technological gadgets (e.g., TVs, computers, cell phones), and these families also report the highest degree of connectivity among their members as opposed to a single-parent family or singles. What is notable about the research is its findings about the content of communication: the communication between parents and their children and with one another focuses on saying hello (74 percent), coordination of schedules (70 percent), and discussion of important matters (42 percent). Cell phone use far exceeds other forms of technological communication such as e-mail or Instant Messaging.

Youth who live in an intricate world of their own — entangled in the web of private feelings, fantasies, queries, agonies, and friendships — certainly welcome new venues for expressing and sharing their world with others. The communication scholars who discuss the effects of technology on communication and behavioral patterns of adolescents agree on at least one effect, and that is the addictive power of technology. I call this effect *technological opium.* Youth talk and make themselves vulnerable through electronic media outlets such as IM, blogs or MySpace sites. They disclose their private selves quite readily, inviting friends and strangers to read revelations that can be inspiring, scandalous, or just plain revealing. However, technology does not drug only the young; the effect on adults is that we interpret our children or grandchildren's obsession to share their inner selves through technology as their unwillingness to do the same with *us.* Yet, as communication scholar and professor Peggy Kendall suggests, "In many ways, IM opens up long-distance relationships to help fill the void many teens feel in their everyday relationships at school and at work."[12] Technological communication does not imply a lack of desire to be intimate with people; on the contrary, it is seen as a medium for involving youth and adults with the lives of others. So the challenge to virtual community is not intimacy or communication itself, but rather the quality of intimacy, the sincerity of community, and the depth of discourse that virtual environments might foster.

Virtual Intimacy

The quality of intimacy is shaped by mutuality, proximity, and authenticity.

Mutuality

Digitally conceived mutuality enables Internet users to share opinions, thoughts, stories, songs, poems, videos, and life in general with one another. Ask adolescents what they love about technology most, and the answer is, "It's fun." Fun is the language of unrealized, unconscious understanding on the adolescent's part of a deeply felt desire for mutuality. Through IM or MySpace, they are involved in the lives of their friends, their friends' friends, and even strangers from around the globe. Being involved in life feels big and encompassing. We grow in mutuality through building bridges to one another. Communication scholars praise IM and MySpace for functioning as a bridge in human relationships. Concretely speaking, digital conversation can help shy kids, kids with low self-esteem, kids who lack assertiveness or confidence, and kids who feel lonely.[13] It bridges gender-based social groups.[14]

Digital mutuality builds upon a mediated communication. The technological medium provides the space and speed that enables such sharing, but it lacks the moral thoughtfulness with which to appreciate and judge this trade in human creativity, vulnerability, and acumen. The tragic case of a Florida teenager who broadcast his suicide via a webcamera illustrates the appalling nature of digital sharing done in a vacuum of ethical responsibility of the viewers.[15] As the young man was dying of a drug overdose, the online discussion of his action concerned how many more pills he needed to terminate his life. A deeply painful personal drama prompted hardly any concerns about how to stop him because in a sense his action was seen as virtual, not real. The Pew Internet and American Life Project research reports that Internet users who share their thoughts, artwork, or photos tend to be subject to cyberbullying more often than those who do not.[16] When the adolescents themselves were asked to explain the reasons for cyberbullying, they suggested three: anonymity (behind-screen machoism), the lack of adult supervision, which can be translated into a lack of moral compass with digital technology, and the belief that online communication is not real.[17] Sharing in virtual space prompts a cyber community to dissociate individuals from their real lives and then feel free to dissect the information they share. What is shared is viewed as another (virtual) dimension of one's life. Because it apparently lacks a real grounding, it can be readily dismissed or ridiculed.

Proximity

Virtual mutuality can be exhilarating, but if it lacks the physical proximity of human relationships, it can feel flat. After a while, the impact of virtual friends whom I never get to see and talk to face-to-face fades.[18] Studying the potential of online communities for growing social capital (i.e., bringing people together and enhancing their togetherness and community involvement), Robert Putnam discusses San Francisco–based web community *Craiglist.org*. Putnam suggests that the success of this online community is due to the fact that it is local and part of the physical life of its users. Spatial proximity enables the users to cultivate their virtual ties in the physical locales (originally the homes, cafes, and parks of San Francisco but now of many other cities too). Putnam argues: "Such use of electronic communication as a supplement (not an alternative) to face-to-face communication may ultimately prove to be the most important effect of the Internet on social connectedness."[19]

The ability to meet in the concrete places of San Francisco and other cities and follow up on the online conversations helps clarify these encounters with bodily clues. Communication scholar Peggy Kendall writes, "One key to successful relationships is an ability to share with one another.... Unfortunately, one of the biggest headaches young people report with IM and other online communication technologies is the ongoing issue of misinterpretation."[20]

Physical proximity frames human discourse and interaction with a degree of security when it comes to interpretation. We can rely on nonverbal clues — such as body language, tone of voice, or even the presence of other people and their interpretive lens when engaged in communication. Physical proximity forces people to pay attention to one another. The absence of it creates freedom to construe identities and social masks that match the profile of a virtual community one is involved with, but not necessarily one's authentic profile. It also enables people to create fictive and idealized perceptions of their virtual buddies. Peggy Kendall sums up the ethereality of cyber relationships with these words: "Unfortunately, online communication technology can also create the *appearance* of relationship, connection, and shared meaning where none truly exists."[21] Our sense of mutuality in a virtual space has an elusive quality. We interact with and attach ourselves to people who feel free to experiment with their sense of self behind the computer screen. Barry Taylor's concept of liquification in the postmodern world suits cyberspace very well because there the lack of gravity enables people to float in the various directions of their fantasies.[22]

The lack of gravity in cyberspace has to do with the lack of proximity. Proximity shapes an individual's understanding of place and identity. It makes us pay attention to geographical boundaries that sequester us (e.g., mountains, cornfields, rivers); to cultural artifacts that define our particular locale (e.g., dialect, clothing, architecture, or customs), to indigenous vegetation and animals. Thus, it confers on us a sense of earthiness or groundedness. As U.S. culture becomes more superficially uniform through chains such as McDonald's, Burger King, and Wal-Mart, it is easy to overlook especially the markers of diversity that expose us to our idiosyncratic physical and cultural genome. We tend to find our identification through chain stores and restaurants that indeed impose a quick and shallow feeling of unity and comfort among people, knowing that a distant town in Texas has the same Wal-Mart inventory as my town in New Jersey.

Place labels us: Positively, it bestows *gravitas* upon us, a sense of being grounded in a particular physical locality that produces seriousness and a sense of trust. A person who wanders too much might project a kind of pioneerism that people misjudge for a restless spirit. Negatively, place can mark us with a scarlet letter. People's value can easily be stymied by the place to which they claim loyalty. The cultural endowment that one inherits from living in a particular place can be both a blessing and a curse. Living in a place challenges us to negotiate between the given, safe, and familiar and the need to grow out of one's place. This means not only leaving a place physically; metaphorically it also means leaving its racial, gender, or economic confines. Ultimately, a place calls for return. Every return to our places of childhood means that we are returning to the well of knowledge. Whether through family values, practices, or experiences, place equips us with knowledge that life outside our locality deepens, tests, or affirms. Thus place functions as an epistemological source for life wisdom in that it juxtaposes our personal, professional identities, relationships, and vocational aspirations to particular soil, houses and graves, traditions and language, memories and imagination, and above all concrete people.

With technology, though, place barely holds any epistemological value. My husband and I were using Skype to talk to my family in Slovakia. After we had finished, Doug forgot to turn off his Skype account. Then the messages kept coming asking him to contact a particular account. Doug asked me: Shall we contact this person? The name of the account gave no clues as to the gender or the place of origin of the person to whom it belonged. I wondered: *Who* are we contacting? Where is this person sitting? Where is his or her home? Michael Bugeja writes that with the computer located in a physical place and e-mail accounts in multiple virtual habitats, the sense of geographical place is blurred[23] — and with it the sense of security and authenticity. Having a place, a home, a locale, writes Quentin Schultze, "is also the setting for *hospitality*, one of the most important neighborly traditions across many cultures."[24] Youth who are heavily immersed in technological locales cannot practice hospitality toward one another. In cyberspace, home hospitality is reduced to adding me as your friend on MySpace or Facebook or to being gracious about my opinions in the chat room. The hospitality of the Internet is the hospitality of some degree of inclusion, but by no means the hospitality of setting a table and preparing a meal.

Authenticity

With the loss of physical mutuality and proximity comes the loss of authenticity. There are two online trends that diminish the authenticity of relationships among youth. The first trend is the trend of befriending.[25] In the Myspace and Facebook worlds, popularity is measured by the number of friends one posts on one's site. Teens seeking acceptance and affirmation from their community of peers frantically chase the numbers. The goal is not to list friends who are trustworthy or genuine; the goal is to impress the community with the bright veneer of apparent popularity. The relationship status box is a way to check who hangs out with whom, who broke up with whom, who is losing his or her traction with the crowds. When youth become uncomfortable with or tired of their online communication, in an instant they can terminate the conversation. In the abounding literature on how technology affects interpersonal skills, scholars point to the loss of the art and courage to interact with people face to face.[26] The *delete* key becomes a new paradigm for how people might handle a conflict. With one click on the relationship status box, teenagers delete their boyfriends or girlfriends or friends who have fallen out of favor. Those who have been "deleted" become spectators of their own relational demise rather than participants in the relationship.

The second trend that affects authenticity is youth coaching themselves into not quite believing what is said online. Fighting against the hurt that comes with misunderstood messages, youth shield themselves with the advice: "Don't take things too seriously when they are said online."[27] The rationale for making up stories or bullying is justified by the technological maxim that says that since online communication is not real, it is okay to say hurtful things. Foolish are those who believe in things said online. Quentin Schultze suggests, "One of the most significant moral dilemmas in cyberspace is how to say what we mean and mean what we say."[28] In his empirical studies with high school adolescents, Chap Clark observed that lying is widely accepted by this population.[29] The mid-adolescents go through a stage that Clark describes as egocentric abstraction.[30] They understand the behavior and actions of the adults as they relate to adolescents, yet their understanding is not nuanced or comprehensive. Youth are sensitive to adults' deception and lies, but their fragile complexity and personal integrity prevent them from assuming full accountability for their own stories and acts of dishonesty. Lacking moral authority, online communication permits ethically lax behavior as opposed to correcting it.

Authenticity is also challenged by the multiple versions of profiles that adolescents post, for example, on their MySpace site. There can be a profile for parents, a profile for real friends, a fantasy profile. Experimentation with personas is part of the individuation process through which youth strive to find their authentic selves. At the same time, profiles are only tentative in their ability to provide an integral sense of one's self. The profiles are also fruits of marketing strategies which quite persistently target the adolescent population. The machine of consumerism exerts massive pressure to reorient an individual toward a specific identity and loyalty to a particular product, lifestyle, or taste. Having a profile means to succumb to the postmodern philosophy of surfaces in which we no longer moor our identities to geographical or vocational stability, but rather to choices and versatility of geographies, professions, and relationships. When the arbiter of personal identity is located in the marketing powerhouse, then one's identity will change correspondingly with the product or idea that is in vogue. Identity in flux is called a profile. The more profiles youth identify with, the less they know of their true selves.

Democratization of Knowledge in Cyberspace

The appeal of virtual community is that it gathers people around the notion of public space or commons. Traditionally, people would congregate in spaces such as a town square to listen to community announcements and talk to one another. Virtual commons are represented by chat rooms, blogs, podcasts, and online communities such as Second Life. Knowledge is shared through online encyclopedias such as Wikipedia, and through Open Source or Course Management Software programs. We can travel the earth via Google Earth. Music lovers can indulge themselves in infinite melodies from the online music library, Napster. Christian believers can gather around Bible study that is ustreamed via webcam from the room of the person who leads it. This is all quite fascinating, of course, opening humankind to an enormous potential of teleporting one another into private spaces, virtual libraries, and commons in order to share and shape knowledge in relationship with others. However, the idea that new virtual media execute democratization of knowledge in Gutenberg's spirit needs to wrestle with a few challenges.

Switch-on Button

First, by providing instant access to information, data, shared virtual forums, and global awareness, the Internet principally and physically does disseminate knowledge but only to those strata of the population who have access to technology or who can afford to pay for it. Economic capital is not the only obstacle to participating in the high-tech world. Living in the high-tech world challenges people to become technologically savvy, which requires a particular set of skills. Learning technological how-to represents the process of socialization into a culture with a distinctive language, values, and techno-practices. Those who master technological competency draw a line between the worlds of the technologically literate and illiterate populations. My mom still wonders at the "miracle" of my being able to access my e-mail account from Slovakia. "But your e-mail account is in the United States," she says in consternation, her perplexity showing me that she connects e-mail with a concrete place — like a landline telephone. If I am out of the concrete locality, I should not be able to access it, she reasons. Regarding Internet technology, my mother is only very slowly developing a conceptual understanding of it due to her lack of images and experiences with technology. When I talk to my nephew and niece about e-mailing, my parents feel excluded. High-tech media inevitably marginalize some family members and further segregate family based on their familiarity with cyberspace or their having economic capital to engage it.

Each in His or Her Own Room

Second, the families who own technology and know how to operate it can live in isolation from one another. Michael Bugeja writes, "Media divide the family via programming, requiring multiple television sets and/or computers so that each member has access to shows or sites of his or her own choosing and, as a consequence, lives apart from others for several hours per day in the same home."[31] Technology has been hijacked by marketing and consumerist agendas, aiming at the partitioning of human communities along lines of buying interests, buying capital, ideological preferences, race and gender preferences, etc. People go to the websites where they feel at home; where they feel that their values, choices, and opinions are shared by other inhabitants of virtual habitats.[32] Catering to individualistic needs and interests, technology "does not bring all people together as much as it fosters the growth of tribal interests, from professional groups to political movements."[33] Michael Pollan in his book *In Defense of*

Food notes an interesting pattern when it comes to family communal meals. The trend is that families who eat meals together do not eat the same meals. Influenced by marketing strategies, the family members eat the food that matches their individual diet. Pollan says, "Kraft or General Mills, for instance, is now determining the portion sizes, not mom, and the social value of sharing food is lost."[34]

When it comes to suggesting which technology has the most isolating effect on families, the Pew Internet and American Life Project research says this: "The Internet has more of a potential than TV to be a solitary activity, isolating household members from one another."[35] The same research proudly points to the fact that even in households with multiple TV sets, family members (especially women and their children or spouses) prefer to watch TV together. Yet, as Putnam's findings indicate, TV watching together diminishes significantly people's investment in the activities that require that family members talk to one another.[36] "Two kids in three aged 8–18 say that TV is usually on during meals in their home."[37] TV watching is declining because of the lure of the Internet. Parents like to go online together with their children; however, surveying cyberspace in family solidarity decreases as children grow into adolescents and become more guarded about their online activities. The Pew Internet and American Life Project argues that as with multiple TVs, so with multiple computers, family members get to interact more with one another.[38] Yet the level of this interaction is typically no more than family members passing and glancing at the screen of another family member, engaging for only a moment before drifting away to the space of their own virtual communities.

I do not want to dismiss too quickly technology's potential for family connectivity. The data show that it indeed contributes to the sense of family connectivity; yet the question is about the quality and the depth of this human togetherness. Talking on a cell phone or peeking over someone's shoulder to see what's up on the Internet does not necessarily generate the intimate connection for which the young long. Robert Putnam's research documents that "the past two decades have witnessed a dramatic change in one traditionally important form of family connectedness — the evening meal."[39] The data from other research suggest a link between the amount of technology and the rate of decline in family meals: simply stated, the less technology a family has, the more communal meal time there is.[40] While technology is praised by its users for enabling them to stay connected with their families and friends, the same users praise it less for its ability to connect them with new people. Thus as a tool that can stretch human connectivity across geographical, economic, racial, or gender boundaries, technology seems to be doing the opposite: it brings people who are close even closer, while leaving strangers at a distance. Technology connects but if connection barely scratches the surface of human longing for intimacy, then in reality it pushes communities apart by usurping quality time in exchange for pseudo-intimacy.

Who Authenticates?

Third, the democratization of knowledge in the era of Gutenberg and the Reformation (especially Martin Luther's part in it) was built upon the notion of the priesthood of all believers. A believer had access to God mediated through his or her belief in Jesus Christ. *Sola Scriptura* and *Sola Fide* liberated believers from the papal claims to the authority of the Word. Luther's reforms empowered believers with their spiritual right to act as arbiters of divine truth; yet this escape toward individualistically based deliberations of biblical authority was tamed by the influence of the church communities. The assembly of the believers, whether they met in churches or houses, balanced too separatist and insular ownership of Scripture on the part of individuals. The communities also affirmed its members in their vocations and proclamations; as such they functioned as nests of support, discernment, and censure. Andrew Pettegree in his book *Reformation and the Culture of Persuasion*, argues that Luther's success as a Reformer can be ascribed to the fact that "Luther

was not presented as a single lonely voice, but as part of a community."[41]

Technology in the United States makes information widely accessible but it lacks the tools to connect information back from the individual receptor to a broader community. In other words, technology is unable to act as a morally imperative and integral force that would bring the information from the extreme and far too distant edges of human interpretation to the center of communal wisdom and hermeneutical guidelines. Quentin Schultze writes, "Cyberculture implicitly defines messaging as *individual* interpretation rather than *shared* interpretation.... [Thus] cyberculture weakens the relationships among messages, communicators, and communities of interpretation."[42]

Is Information Knowledge?

Fourth, technology distributes information, not knowledge. Information is instant, rational, and impersonal. Knowledge, on the other hand, is a long-term practice of growing in life experiences, intuiting life complexities, and immersing oneself in relationships. It is a practice of weaving the narrative of place and time in relationship to self, community, and universe. Living a sequestered life in technological habitats leads to a person's displacement in the ecology of living relationships, says Bill Plotkin.[43] His concern is especially with our young, for too much reliance on technology to acquire knowledge diminishes a person's resourcefulness and creativity to grow in the understanding of life. For a child who is learning how to belong, ecoliteracy — that is, knowledge accrued in the ecosystems of humans, animals, and plants — is an essential prerequisite for a later comprehensive knowledge of life.

Technology builds on the democratization of relationships and knowledge as a fundamental paradigm through which it operates when shaping human communities, their values, knowledge of life, and work patterns. Its goal in formation is to enhance democratic governance of human societies by providing citizens with high-tech tools to spread and participate in democracy. (These tools can range from military arsenals to machinery as a substitute for farm animals to computerized voting.)[44] Technology attempts to foster democratic discourse by suggesting that it has a real potential for being a habitat of human genuineness, acceptance, and truth. It also claims to be an open flow of resources such as shared knowledge, personal creativity, advice, or information. Indeed, the Internet itself is a huge warehouse of pooled human wisdom that provides tips on how to cook a turkey or clean a shirt collar as well as an encyclopedic mapping of history, people's diaries, and the latest news. It is also a huge warehouse for selling and trading merchandise — a virtual alternative to Moroccan bazaars. The Internet organizes itself around these two basic principles of society: economy and community. Technology, whether it is a washing machine or the Internet, challenges us to realize that partnering with it leads to new patterns of social structure.[45] The greatest challenge to technology, however, is its inability to integrate itself into the ecology of living systems that tie our planet together. Technology is *not* a living organism. It absorbs life from its inhabitants and users, but it cannot generate life on its own. Being lifeless, it does not have the ability to create what Schultze would call the virtues of the heart.

As a result, technology distributes techniques for the mind, but not practices of the heart.[46] The practices of the heart help human beings transcend their finitude by creating encounters with the divine. They prepare us to receive the holy presence, inciting vulnerability and the openness of the human soul to the purifying and transforming work of the Holy Spirit. The practices of the heart grow in communities that celebrate, practice, and themselves evolve around their encounters with the Trinitarian God. The life that these communities fashion for their members represents an ecology of being — embodied in the breath of divine creation, thus interrelated to living contexts such as earth, people, fauna and flora, and, above all, the Creator. The communities I talk about are primarily two: church and family. They are natural habitats for creating, sustaining, and commissioning their young. They are generative sources of spiritual practices, values, and directions for how to live a life that integrates one's faith with one's role in society. They anchor children and youth in tangible representations of love, care, and nurture.

Embodied Communities and Embodied Practices

Virtual mutuality, proximity, and authenticity stand in contrast to their embodied realities. However, previrtual generations can compare and contrast communication and behavior patterns or the quality of intimacy because they have a point of reference. Young Americans who grow up in high-tech culture evaluate communities or family closeness through a lens of techno experience.[47] Techno experience acting as a dominant interpretative lens of communal life, communication, or behavioral patterns provides a myopic view of what life is or could be. Not knowing or not practicing alternatives to many of the virtual modes of life, the young will live lives like those in the movie *Matrix* (which shows what it means to live in virtual captivity). A kitchen table ministry of formation by contrast presents opportunities, creates practices, and generates experiences of embodied and shared intimacy. For example, mutuality is shared in handing to one another the plates and the meal; proximity becomes real in sitting close to one another, and authenticity grows evident in (and is tested by) faces, tone of voices, gestures, etc. Fred Edie argues that "The body is the context through which we become present to God."[48] From the nest of embodied human togetherness, a youth can embark on the journey of finding a place in the global community. As a human being embodied in a particular body, family, and physical place, a youth has contexts in which to encounter the divine. The challenge of postmodern culture is its liquification, which means that experiences, feelings, or ties do not have moorings. To experience the divine one needs "earthiness," a context that can absorb and be filled in with the holy presence. Sensitizing youth to their encounters with the divine calls for embodied ways of being. This translates into nurturing youth in the practices, routines, and discourses that set loose their spiritual and vocational imagination, yet tie their dreams to a particular place.

Vocation

Adolescence is about being sent forth. This means that adolescents are eager to fashion a vision for their individual and communal future. Bill Plotkin frames the generative questions of this stage in terms of focus on society and social life. During adolescence, says Plotkin, "the world becomes more personally *constructed* and *chosen*, as opposed to the given world of family and nature that was *discovered* and *accepted* [in childhood]."[49] Adolescents intentionally shift their energy to the outside social and communal dimensions of existence in hopes of finding answers to cosmic questions like the meaning of life and death. Questions about one's vocation enter this stage of life with a sense of urgency. The need to authenticate one's life in terms of a mandate and purpose that adolescents intuit and seek to materialize has them reach outward — out of their community of birth to the communities of possibilities, ideals, potential answers, and instruction. A youth's hunger for being commissioned and integrated into a grand scheme of things is not adequately validated by consumer and materialist society. Giving youth a driving permit or permission to drink alcohol is not of the same caliber as the privilege to vote. We as a society honor youth's zeal on the level of permits, but not at the level of privileges. A privilege makes youth aware of the substantive change in the relationships to oneself, one's family, or one's country. A permit slides youth into the adult world and its behaviors without cultivating a qualitative leap in understanding about what authenticity, personal integrity, and spiritual wholeness might mean.

Bestowing privilege means conferring dignity upon the human spirit and its growth. The history of the Christian church shows examples of the church's efforts to synchronize the developmental progression of youth with spiritual progression. The liturgical rites of passage such as confirmation are performed in order to signify youth's physical and mental changes as stately and venerable. In the Roman Catholic tradition confirmation is viewed as sacrament. It is through sacraments that — for example — a scholastic theologian of the High Middle Ages, Thomas Aquinas, drew parallels between the physical and spiritual life of a person. In his commentary on the sacraments, Aquinas explains where he sees the parallel: A person comes into life by *generation* (i.e., by birth) and experiences *progression* in his or her development through physical growth and food that sustains his or her life, and finally through *healing* that restores health.[50] The seven sacraments follow and address the stages of individual life. For example, *baptism* addresses birth, the spiritual growth and the stage of maturity are marked by *confirmation, the Eucharist* satisfies spiritual hunger, disease and sin are alleviated by the sacrament of *penance*, and so forth.[51]

For Aquinas, three sacraments in particular promote the spiritual life of a person: baptism, confirmation, and Eucharist. Out of these three, the sacrament of confirmation addresses the stage of human life at which a person is capable of performing mature human acts and reaches spiritual maturity. In the physical sense this stage of life equates to completed physical growth (a person has reached an erect stature and his or her muscles and bones are essentially formed.) The question is, What exactly is spiritual maturity, and what does it require one to do? Spiritual maturity requires that a person think and act virtuously.[52] In Cristina Traina's interpretation, Aquinas associates these faculties with a person's "capacity to reason, including the ability to make and act on responsible choices."[53] The implications are that spiritual maturity follows rather closely the trajectory of human mental development. At the stage of spiritual maturity, one defines one's

personal relationship with Christ in broader terms, as membership in Christ's body, where one's individual dimension of faith
incorporates itself into the faith of the church.

In confirmation, a young believer is incorporated into a larger
spiritual body of Christians by professing faith publicly and
declaring readiness to stand against sin. Confirmation represents
the rite of initiating a young believer into a greater cause. In
the Protestant tradition confirmation is not a sacrament. In the
Lutheran tradition confirmation is both a rite and a practice. As
a rite, it affirms one's baptism through one's understanding and
professing baptismal faith. As a practice, it acts upon the baptismal mandate as the confirmands are commissioned to take their
profession of baptismal faith to the ministry of active witness in
the congregation and in the world. The mandate of baptism carries the public dimension of confirmation as advocated by the
scholastics. Baptismal faith that is professed at confirmation acts
as a response of the individual to God's gift of grace through
Christ. As such confirmation is viewed as a life-long process
instead of a one-time event. Through confirmation as baptismal
ministry, a youth manifests progress from an individual embrace
of faith (in which faith acts as a means for a believer's personal
salvation) to embracing community and its needs (in which faith
acts as a believer's readiness to service and commitment to others).
As an ecclesiastical practice, it is confirmation that captures the
hunger of youth for belonging in a grand style — now as members
of the adult community who are commissioners of God's saving
work both in the congregation and in the world.

Being part of the living ecology of faith, kitchen table youth
ministry nurtures youth in this understanding of their baptismal
mandate. This ministry seeks to nurture a youth's understanding
of "what God is calling me to do in my life" through experience of
theological reflection around the table. Both the kitchen and the
Eucharistic table host the Word that in its sovereignty speaks out
through human agents. At both tables the Word invites its hearers
to enter the story of God's action in the world, and to proclaim

this story boldly. Taking part in the Eucharistic story, as an actor takes part in a dramatic performance, counteracts what Fred Edie calls a reductionist view of the Eucharist among youth.[54] Instead of seeing the Eucharist as a mere mnemonic device, tThe act of opening memories through the Word has a deeper spiritual significance: It is a pathway to experiencing the past and bringing it alive. In the Eucharist, God's Word unleashes the reality of deliverance, grace, and nurture because when God proclaims his Word, this Word becomes a live reality (e.g., as in Genesis 1:3: "Then God said, 'Let there be light; and there was light.'") Combining remembrance with proclamation, we make the Word come alive. The Eucharist combines the power of memories with the power of proclamation into an experiential encounter with the power of the living God through the Spirit. Orchestrated by the Holy Spirit, our lives reenact and embody the Eucharistic themes.

Kitchen table ministry is also a ministry of remembering, experiencing, and embodying Eucharistic themes of divine love and care. When a family sits down for a meal, it puts flesh on commitment to its young. It enacts the stable presence of adults in children's lives, manifests nurture, and translates love into tangibles such as table talk, time for one another, and physical nearness. I argue that a family table anchors the young in the experience of the Eucharistic table. The sacramental presence of Christ is invoked through the practice of the meal, the corporeality of the church body is reenacted around the home table, and the promises of God are echoed in the rituals of family closeness, story time, and giving.

Sending youth forth means loosening adults' grip on young people's vocational aspirations and allowing them to dream their place in the Kingdom of God. As with the Eucharistic table — which prompts a release in the spiritual imagination of believers to grasp the past and envision the future — so the family table needs to empower youth to be visionaries of their call. This means that a table has practices in which faith stories, life stories, and bold metaphors can evoke youth's openness to the Holy Spirit. It is to these that I turn in the next chapter.

You can continue kitchen table youth ministry by:

✦ *Counting your electronic gadgets*

I encourage every family to count the electronic gadgets it owns. Focus on the pattern of togetherness by also counting the hours that your family spends together when using them. If it helps, keep a quick log on your refrigerator for everybody to see. You do not have to be precise: estimate. Focus questions might include:

1. Does TV watching bring your family together? If so, how much time of togetherness does this activity allocate to your family?

2. What about surfing the Internet or talking on the cell phone with your family members? Try to establish the activity connected with technology that gives your family the most time together. Compare it with what I call embodied activities, such as household chores, traveling by car, hiking, sports, or shopping.

✦ *Using technology to initiate conversation with your teenage children*

1. Using data from the previous analysis, suggest that your teenage children give you time for face-to-face conversation every week proportional to the total time they spend in virtual conversations. Ask teenagers themselves to suggest how much proportional time they should spend in face-to-face conversations with their family. Try it for a week, making persons involved aware about their time spent in virtual vis-à-vis embodied communication.

2. Use electronic media to continue your relationship and conversation with your teenage children. Their ability to navigate high-tech media often surpasses that of their parents, and they are for the most part willing to help, instruct, show, or tutor their parents, grandparents, or aunts (in my case).

3. Ask probing questions: During opportune moments, invite your teenagers to show you how Facebook works and how they get their friends. Ask them: What do they think about having a high number of virtual friends whom they cannot possibly get to know? Have they come across cyberbullying? in what form? what is their response to it? Use the Internet with your children to do educational research, for example, to learn how much of the world has access to the Internet. Is the Internet really a global medium of communication? How many people is your teenager chatting with, e-mailing, or text-messaging who come from different parts of the globe?

Chapter Three

The Practice of Table Talk:
Tell Me a Story

N OT EVERY WEEKEND, but quite regularly, my parents, my brother, and I would visit my aunt and her family. We would gather for a Sunday meal around a large, oak table in what was my aunt's living and dining room. Around the table, my family would exchange their accounts about what had happened to whom in town, remember their youthful years, recall anecdotes about family members who were no longer among us, complain about the politicians and the high cost of living, and always discuss the church. As a child, I used to retire to a comfortable sofa in the corner of the room after we had finished the main meal, and there, cuddled with my older sibling and cousins, I continued to listen to the adults' table talk. The pastor of my family's congregation and other guests from the community would also be invited to join us on occasion. As a youth, I was particularly interested in the theological talk between the pastor and my family. I tried to participate in the discussion, mainly in the form of asking curious questions and sometimes offering youthful philosophical insights in my attempt to crack the nut of life's complexities.

So if you were to ask me, "How were you nurtured in faith?" I would answer: In the church and around the table. Reflecting back on my family's table talk, I believe that *something* formative happened around that table. The large oak table provided the opportunity to be with one another as family. We gathered for more than food: for stories, for laughter, for argument, for sharing in human joy and sadness. We gathered for human fellowship. And at the center of that human fellowship was the story.

Table Fellowship as Instruction in Christian Faith

In this book I propose kitchen table ministry as a model of family catechesis in the twenty-first century. During the Reformation period it was Martin Luther who pioneered family catechesis as a model of relational instruction in the Christian faith. He taught that it was a parental responsibility to educate one's children in the basics of faith. Gerald Strauss suggests that "the family's fellowship in Christian instruction was the heart of Luther's evangelical program in his early years as a reformer."[1] The practices of faith that a family in Luther's time would employ included not only readings from the Bible, catechism, and prayers; the parents were also expected to model the Christian faith to their children through their pious behavior. A family's practices of appropriating the Word of God into its daily routine helped the children become accustomed to interacting with the Word. The value of family catechesis lies in the fact that the intimate spiritual relationship between God and a person can be experienced and reenacted through family relationships centered on God's Word.[2]

The guiding formative practice of family catechesis is table fellowship. Table fellowship acts as an embodied practice, that is, it is tied to a particular activity such as having a dinner and the experience that this activity forms in its participants. Having dinner embodies a divine praxis of care, hospitality, remembering, and retelling the story. As Christian believers we participate in this divine praxis when gathering around the Eucharistic tables of grace. We re-create this divine praxis at our dinner tables. Practical theologian Don Browning stresses the importance of reenacting the liturgical life of the church at home for the sake of a greater family cohesion. He says, "When home rituals and the liturgies of church or synagogue reinforce each other, family life is made more cohesive and integrated more completely into the wider community. . . . Family rituals at the dinner table, before bed, and on trips correlate with the effective communication of family traditions."[3] In the context of twenty-first century catechesis, kitchen table fellowship stands for an initiation rite into the community of the faithful, its identity, practices, and stance. By weaving the threads of personal narratives into a pattern of meaning and belonging in a Christian metanarrative, a family forms an identity that is based in the story of grace, vocation, and God's presence in their very lives.

Sitting at the Table with Martin Luther

During the High Middle Ages, Martin Luther's table talks engaged in a tradition of storytelling similar to that of the familiar legends about saints, kings, and heroic warriors.[4] Valued more as a piece of literature than as a historically factual and theologically well argued treatise, Martin Luther's *Table Talk* provides us with the "opinions, the motives, the reading, the daily life and personal attitude of the greatest German of his age."[5] *Table Talk* covers a variety of topics on which Luther commented in casual conversations with his guests. They range from justification and free will to marriage, education, the arts, and other topics. The tradition of such table talk started in the context of Luther dictating his biblical interpretations to his guests. Soon enough, his disciples started recording not only Luther's theological comments, but the informal conversations around them too. In his distinguished career as a church reformer, Luther's reflections on life proved to be the gems of wisdom and experience that Luther's guests found valuable enough to write down. Being invited to Luther's table was a matter of honor, and young theology students got their seats on the recommendations of their mentors, and spoke of it as a privilege. The participants at these table talks observed that there were no topics about which Luther would be hesitant to talk. He was frank and open about his life. His sense of humor, jovial mood, making jokes, and teasing his wife were as characteristic of Luther's companionship style as were his moodiness, brooding thoughts, and silence around the table. When discussions grew heated, Luther's effort to maintain decency and respect among the participants intensified accordingly.

There are several characteristics of Luther's table fellowship that can be transposed into the contemporary context of American families, for example, hospitality, storytelling, conversation, privileged time, the honor of being around the table, reflections on the issues of life and faith. Three characteristics in particular stand in contrast to virtual fellowship: physical communication and hospitality, embodied authority (both in the Scripture and in the physicality of human agents), and the authenticity of storytelling. These characteristics help shape a table fellowship into a practice for instructing children and youth in the Christian faith. The generative power of table talk to catechize the family lies in its relationality — relationality grounded in concrete space and through concrete practices.

Table Talk: Introduction to Narrative Catechesis

Family catechesis of the twenty-first century unfolds as a process of creating a narrative identity of the family and its members. Stories help the family to articulate its family identity and to confer on family the sense of name that binds the unit in its understanding of who it is, where it came from, and what its historic mandate is. The research on identity construction in families suggests that "families not only have a sense of what might be called 'familyness' but also language (in this case, storytelling) plays a pivotal role in maintaining and expressing this familyness."[6] The immense popularity of the StoryCorps project, a mobile booth that travels across the country and gives all generations the opportunity to record their life stories, demonstrates a real need of human beings to tell a story as well as to be a part of a larger story.[7] In the words of the StoryCorps founder, Dave Isay, the stories that people eagerly record convey the truth that "we are not just a nation of celebrity worship and consumption but rather a people defined by our character, courage, and heart."[8] When a StoryCorps booth arrives in a city, there are only so many slots available. It is a privilege to tell one's story.

Storytelling is a formative practice in that it envokes connection, group identity, and imagination; it also helps preserve tradition, membership, and the sense of being placed in a particular time and location. Maureen O'Brien, building upon sociological research by Robert Wuthnow, underscores storytelling as a dominant and favorite mode of communication in small groups — and therefore a "natural" for youth and families.[9] When authors Dori Baker and Joyce Mercer interviewed youth from the Youth Theological Initiative at Candler School of Theology in Atlanta, they observed that youth regarded the personal interviews with them to be one of the favorite features of their summer program.[10] Youth enjoyed the interviewing process because they felt that the adults took time to show their interest in what youth thought and the stories they had to share. Sharing a story is a practice that assists in creating an atmosphere of trust and bonding within a family. With regard to youth, it reemphasizes the interest that family members have in one another. "Story," as Sarah Arthur argues, "does not equal fiction. . . . Its subject matter is human experience."[11] Therefore sharing stories that embody a collective human experience of life and of relationships to the world, to one another, and to God can help nurture young people's desire to be part of a grand scheme.

Yet, as Dave Isay concludes from his work of facilitating and recording people's stories, "It takes courage to walk into a StoryCorps booth."[12] Sharing a story is an act of bravery because it calls people to bequeath meaning and purpose to their feelings, thoughts, experiences, and life events. It is an exercise in creating a narrative identity — an organizing principle for seeing life as a coherent and meaningful whole. It is also an exercise in theological reflection by which one uses the vernacular of everyday life to interpret the metaphors of divine presence. Telling a story means describing life in the vernacular. It means describing its ordinariness, its banality, and its brevity only to unveil how charged with depth these life moments are. Teaching the complexity of life, endurance of faith, and mystery of God in Christ starts with teaching our children to listen to a story and to tell a story.

When Martin Luther Is Not Sitting at the Table with Us....

Each family can very well find its own questions that initiate their theological discussions. However, parents tend to be hesitant about reading the Bible with their children or talking about faith issues with them. Those families who do not have specific theological training feel ill-equipped to be spiritual mentors to their children, and they gladly pass the torch of spiritual formation to professionals in the church. Martin Luther is not sitting at the table with us, yet the absence of biblical scholarship or theological training among the family members ought not to permit the absence of God-talk. Theologian Gordon Kaufman claims that doing theology is a human task whose goal is to construct the image of God.[13] Human beings attempt the task by seeking the metaphors and symbols by which they capture the images of God. The metaphors are extrapolated from human experiences, reflections on the human condition and nature as recorded in the Bible, tradition, and personal narratives. Being a theologian involves being imaginative and alert to manifestations of God's revelations of God-self through finitude (such as human life), creation (such as nature and cosmos) and transcendence (such as death and resurrection of Jesus Christ). The absolute divine revelation for Christians is of course embodied in Jesus Christ. In Christ God not only reveals the salvation plan for fallen humanity, but God also takes on the bodily form that allows human beings to identify with the absolute God through God's humanness in Jesus Christ. Although one can dismiss the need for theological training, one should not dismiss the need for identifying the images through which God in Christ meets and claims us. Kaufman insists that "We are the ones...who must construct the conception of God which will be meaningful and significant for our day. There is simply no one else to do it."[14]

The implications of his assertion for spiritual formation are urgent. In truth, the task of spiritual formation summons individuals to an honest and painstaking search for God. It calls persons to embark on a laborious journey of looking for the obvious God amid human experience while learning to embrace the mystery of God at the same time. It means a call to understanding, feeling, intuiting, and narrating God's revealing and God's hidden presence in one's life. This call is perhaps articulated most loudly by narrative theology. Through the lens of narrative theology, doing theology represents going back to an original source or means of expression that captures God's activity in the world, such as lived experience, story, or myth.[15] Narrative theologians move from theological reflection expressed mainly through a propositional and abstract language to one that is intuited, imagined, and embedded in the story. William Bausch, a narrative theologian, argues that "all theologies . . . must somehow tap into and reflect life and point to story, and all stories are ultimately theological."[16]

The theological character of stories lies in their ability to initiate theological reflection. Theological reflection is like a conversation among one's life, its questions, its meaning, and the divine presence. With passing time, stories transform themselves from being individually owned experiences of life into shared reflections upon universal themes and virtues such as life, death, love, pain, morality. When personal memories fade, stories continue to amass conversational themes that transcend sociohistorical contingencies of human existence (time, language, culture, space). Stories, as religious educator Mary Elizabeth Moore argues, "can embrace considerable complexity and weave characters and events together in a way that communicates relationships more fully than most categorical and conceptual language can do."[17] The fruit of theological reflection is the skillful negotiation between lived human reality and divine reality as recorded in the Bible. Conversation between biblical story and personal story is a fundamental training ground in which we practice the skill of negotiation — by understanding the meaning of the biblical and personal stories, asking questions, struggling with the answers, looking for parallels, and dreaming in metaphors.

At the same time I do not want to give the impression that such conversation does not draw on the creedal and dogmatic tradition of the Christian faith. Human experience as the source of divine metaphors (both positive and negative) needs to be balanced with the testimony of Scripture and the creedal tradition of the Christian church. In fact, our engagement with the tradition is necessary since locating God solely in human experience does not yield fruits of redemption or knowledge of God's activity in history in its totality. An abused or ill-treated child has a hard time seeing the image of a loving God in a malevolent adult. A child whose parent dies will not experience his or her parent's resurrection, but the belief in the bodily resurrection of Christ and all the souls who are with Christ might bring some hope to a grieving teenager. Dogmatic and creedal traditions of the Christian church express truths about God in Jesus Christ that are of limited accessibility to human experience or are mysterious to it (e.g., resurrection). Catechetical instruction in the congregations (e.g., Sunday school, confirmation preparation, and youth groups) offers basic literacy in biblical, creedal, and liturgical traditions of various denominations, and therefore constitutes a vital component of narrative theology by substantiating it in the tradition of the Christian church.

What We Do as Narrative Theologians

When the guests gathered for meals and conversation around Luther's table, they wanted to engage Luther on theological issues. In bringing questions and stories from their own lives, guests were in effect expressing their desire to hear Luther's biblical and theological perspective on them. As narrative theologians we share life stories with our young. We take our stories, questions, and dilemmas to a scriptural story to have our lives be illuminated by God's Word and God's Word be contested by our stories, questions, and dilemmas. In doing so, we implicitly seek our place in the universe and strive to define our relationship with the Trinitarian God.

In order to enter into conversation with the Christian story, we need to own a personal story. Through a personal story we can engage the biblical story in a much more authentic and complex way than we can engage the dogmatic teachings of the church because we build our connection in the rich soil of shared experiences of people from the past. In contrast to doctrinal articulation of theological truths, a biblical story conveys theological essentials by naming a particular human experience. This experience — whether it is of suffering as in the book of Job or of God's sacrificial love for humanity expressed in the death of Jesus Christ — serves as a point of reference for our own experiences in relation to tradition, the present, and God in Christ. The biblical stories testify to relationships between God and God's creation. God's intentions, patterns of care, and interaction with human beings can be complex and ambiguous, but most important, the stories that narrate divine reality in the Bible are our stories, too.

Storytelling circle

The Christian story dares us to account for its ambiguity and complexity, which means that — as narrative theologians — we read and narrate it with honesty. This further means that our narrating God's activity in the Bible is an act of audacity to face up to Godself. I am convinced that the practice that assists in this theological narrating is the practice of table talk and that this consists of three movements: (1) owning and naming one's own experience; (2) engaging one's experience with the world; and (3) placing one's experience in the conversation with the narratives of Scripture. These movements compose a storytelling circle that generates theological reflection. Let me illustrate these movements with the following example: My narrating of God's activity begins with my personal experience. My personal experience is such that I went through a family tragedy during which I lost my only brother who was a son, a husband, and a father to two children. I call this first movement a lament. As a lament this experience makes me engage the world with heightened sensitivity to human pain, suffering, and personal relationships. It urges me to invite into my life the experiences of lament of other family members, people from other communities, or works of art that serve as a lens for my own scriptural engagement (movement 2). Placing my experience into a conversation with Scripture (in my case a sermon I heard) represents movement 3 and closes the storytelling circle.

Here is the story: In the summer of 2007, my husband and I moved to a new geographical area. As new residents, we were looking for a church community. On a bright, warm summer morning we entered an enthusiastic, energetic congregation. The church band played up-beat music, people were clapping their hands and projected happiness and joy. The lyrics of the songs that were played said something to the effect that life with Jesus was sweet and that walking with Jesus made us happy. The sermon continued with the message that Christian life was a happy existence. The message stopped me in my tracks. For that same summer, just a couple of months before we visited this church, another tragedy had struck my family. I was thinking about my teenage nephew who was a regular churchgoer — just like the youth in the church band — obedient to God's commands and eager for God's Word, yet who had a hard time believing that God was not a mean-spirited deity for having taken away his father that summer. That summer, the moment when Martin had heard that an ambulance was rushing to the crash scene, he kneeled down and prayed with all his soul that God save his father's life. As Martin continues to read the Bible and pray, he senses the truth that there is more to one's life with Jesus than sweetness and happiness or answered prayers. I read Matthew 8: "For everyone who asks receives, and everyone who searches finds, and for everyone who knocks, the door will be opened," and I *know* that Martin had not received what he was asking for in the moment of his utmost spiritual vulnerability. He will have to reckon with the silence of God at that particular moment for the rest of his life.

Going through the steps of the storytelling circle yields the following results: First, it points out the aspects of the Word that are ambiguous and require further reflection. Concretely speaking, the storytelling circle that originated with juxtaposing my particular human experience with the Scripture gave rise to a new metaphor for divine presence in my life and possibly my nephew's: a hidden and enigmatic God.

Second, the experience opened me and possibly will open my nephew to the mystery of the divine Word, and to the fact that the answers it provides are the beginning of the spiritual quest rather than the resolution of it.

Third, it yields an honest conversation between human experience and the Word that brings out the complexity of Christian existence. Elaborating on this point, this further means that one is able to expose simplistic or literal readings of biblical texts in our churches and indict and correct theologies that are not true to human life. We can pronounce a verdict: When the church relaxes its commitment to teach, sing, and preach the gospel authentically, it trivializes human life. It spins life into a romance in which everything turns out good with God's help, and it spins the gospel into a practical guide to a believer's successful and happy life.

Contrary to an idealistic approach to the Bible that we employ in order to dismiss the messiness of its texts or to speak over its burdensome silence with a pretentious hope, there is a conversational approach. Religious educator Carol Lakey Hess defines this approach as one by which we converse with the Bible and its texts, wrestle with it, even talk back to it.[18] Our experience becomes our voice with which to carry on an honest conversation. Therefore, if we take human experience and human story as a basis for communicating and engaging the Word, our lives will be bound in a dialectical relationship between the depth of understanding and the depth of mystery, between the depth of grace and the depth of judgment, and between the depth of love and the depth of pain. Such life resembles much more closely the life of Christian discipleship than the life lived without ambiguities.

Being in conversation about God means being in conversation with one another

Narrative theology emphasizes theological reflection originating with human experience, which serves as a magnifier of divine presence in a person's life. Human experience of life that is imparted through story and in the context of table fellowship represents a unique opening for families and their young to engage the matters of faith, God, or good and evil. Stories offer a softer entry point to talking with youth about faith than does memorization of a creedal tradition. Employing story as a catechetical tool means that our conversations about God begin as conversations about ourselves. These can be rich and complex because story-sharing erects a reflective framework within which families and youth can safely wrestle with the dissonances of life and faith.

Narrating life in a conversational manner is a skill of both imagination and courage. It is also a manifestation of care for one another. Conversational caring is a premise of care, referred to by Carol Lakey Hess, in which we manifest care by initiating a hard dialogue. "Going deep," argues Hess "where we probe beneath the surface, where we question the way things are, and where it sometimes gets uncomfortable, is crucial for genuine relationality and mature caring."[19] Descent to the depths of human earnestness requires preparation. Bottomless and hard conversations surface the truth of human experience. But without an environment that is able to hold it, such truth can destroy, not transform, human rapport. Throughout this book I argue for a practice that helps grow environments of trust, familiarity, and confidence to be truthful without riposte. This practice is table talk, the assets of which are physical proximity, regularity, and talk.

Dinner Talk

When a family sits down for a meal, it adds a vital beat to the life that pulses with energy, work, and schedules. The life-sustaining beat in the form of a family meal secures regularity of physical presence, nurture, and talk among family members. Regularity leads to familiarity, familiarity leads to confidence, and confidence leads to being a bard. Communication scholar Shoshana Blum-Kulka argues that regular participation of children and youth at meals and during a meal's conversation helps them develop narrative skills, the ability to discern appropriate topics for talk, and the familiarity with the cultural rules guiding the discourse.[20] Dinnertime functions both as a sociable and socializing event. In its sociable function, dinnertime fosters community and family togetherness. It provides an opportunity for the individual members of the family to speak in an unstructured way. Its focus is on open and spontaneous conversation that builds up sharing, relationships, and solidarity with one another. In its socializing function dinnertime concerns itself with pursuing a certain goal. For example, dinnertime can be viewed as an initiation rite into adult discourse and rules for its conduct. Or it can be seen as a vehicle for transmitting information, instruction, or family values. Dinner talks usually combine both functions and do not draw rigid boundaries between sociability and the socializing aspect.

Using dinner conversation as an entry point into faith discussion with youth builds on the socializing aspect of dinner, of getting youth involved with the questions of the faith tradition. Obviously, the hard part is to figure out how to structure a dinner conversation so that it leads to engagement with faith, the Bible, or a Christian lifestyle. Luther would start his meal conversations with a question: "What's the news?"[21] This remains a valid entry point to dinner conversations in the twenty-first century also. The focus that this type of question brings out is that of action. Individual family members inquire from one another about the "action news" from school, work, neighborhood, or the sports field. The action news framework belongs to a category of immediate family concerns, and it implies a special entitlement or privilege to tell a story.[22] In other words, having a story to tell or being asked to tell a story is a means of power by which individuals establish their right to participate in the conversation and to be considered members of the group. In addition to action stories, conversations can be filled in by family fables, which are classified as nonimmediate family concerns.[23] Entry points to this type of conversation are facilitated by a family guest or by references to various artifacts, such as family album, or a family joke, or a phrase. Telling a story means sharing a personal experience. (The time and space in which a personal experience occurred are not as relevant to the actual time of telling as is the case with the action-news framework.) This experience can be shared in the monologic mode or polyphonic mode, meaning shared mode.[24] Families tend to do better when they tell their stories in a polyphonic mode, presenting the stories as "we-family." This enables children and youth to have a joined ownership of the story and feel they are equal participants in the discourse and the family unit.

What Parents Say and What Teenagers Hear

Dinner meals are important sociable and socializing events but their formative effect changes when children become adolescents. The reason for this is that it can be quite difficult to have a dinner with a teenage child. Even if a teenager is able to be at home and not at a soccer practice, realistically most family meals with teenagers are far from being ballads on a day in the life of a teenager. Instead, youth can be curt, unwilling to say much, and quick to leave the family table. Writes Michael Riera, "Seldom is the dinner table the site of meaningful information exchange and value clarification, as it was several years ago when your child was still in grade school."[25] Teenage sons and daughters do not easily volunteer their deep thoughts at mealtime, especially if the meal time serves as a short pause to fuel one's body for the family's hectic routine.

What, then, is the value of family dinners for communicating with teenage children? I call for a dinnertime to be the time during which a family re-creates for its members a sanctuary from the stressful demands of everyday work or school life. It ought to be a time of opportunity to see how family members are doing. Clues of a difficult day, conflict with a boss or friends, exhaustion, success and accomplishments, can all be spotted during dinner. Therefore it is important for families to establish time for eating together that does not feel like a drive-through McDonald's experience. Studies on family conversations that occur at dinner note that families often start by telling each other about the events of their day. Children are encouraged to share with their parents what happened to them during their day; mothers usually share about their day more often and openly than fathers do. Families use this type of communication to debrief one another on assignments, schedules, parties, future planning, and simply checking in on one another. It may be that no story is told during a family meal, but that does not mean the meal is a failure. For a family meal and table talk represent a means of welcome to a more heartfelt and in-depth talk that might occur later on. For example, my nephew loves to talk and share stories with his mother at bedtime. Although he does not say much during meal times, seeing his family together on a regular basis creates a trustworthy relationship with his mother and leads him to open up with her later on in the evening.

When David Isay tried to document what life looks like during a week lived in an impoverished neighborhood in Chicago, he delegated recording to two boys from the neighborhood. He says about one of them: "The microphone had given LeAlan the license to ask questions he had never asked before — about the father he never knew, about his mother's mental illness, about his grandmother's childhood. The interview opened up lines of conversation between LeAlan and his grandmother."[26] Family dinner and table talk strive to open up lines of communication between youth and their families. They act for teenage children as ways to cement trust and reliance in the presence of adults. Hard talks are artful practices of gender, place, and time-based negotiations. They occur around the table, in the car, or at one's teenage child's bedside. But the commitment to talk, to ask questions, to be concerned, and to listen is a prerequisite to all. The primary place to practice it is around the table and the family meal.

Talking with Girls and Talking with Boys

Parent-daughter patterns of communication

In her research on the patterns of conversation between men and women and mothers and daughters, Deborah Tannen observes that talk is an essential apparatus for forging intimacy and closeness between mothers and their daughters.[27] In volunteering details of each other's lives, mothers and daughters reinstate their emotional, bodily, and spiritual proximity from a maternal womb to a medium of conversation. These conversations are usually both deeply endearing and dangerously volatile. As the daughter begins the process of individuation in her teenage years, her need to establish the autonomous self pulls her toward a freedom that remains with her throughout the adult years. A mother-daughter conversation takes on the means of expressing the struggle between a continuous intimacy and care that a daughter desires to have and a mother desires to give *and* freedom from too much closeness and love.

With mothers hoping to hold power over their daughters and daughters hoping to gain control over their lives, the conversations during adolescence can turn into verbal dynamite.[28] Quite regular outbursts of explosive conversations between teenage daughters and their parents represent only one end of the relationship; on the other end is the inevitable desire to be connected and intimate with one's parents. Tannen researches that intimacy is best achieved by keeping up with details of a child's life.[29] This involves knowing your daughter's or son's friends' names, regular activities he or she is involved with, eating habits, fashion styles, etc. It sounds like an "of-course-I-know-it-all" task, but it is not so simple. Social websites like Facebook and MySpace document the speed with which these givens can change. Friends, styles, values, or planned parties evolve rapidly in virtual space where social networking occurs these days. Keeping up with broken alliances and new loyalties of a teenage child is a task that requires speediness of a parent's eye and a quick reaction time.

In order to establish connection with their family members, women use what Tannen calls troubles talk.[30] A mother chooses to talk about her day in terms of challenges, difficult tasks, or overcoming obstacles to solicit empathy and compassion, but above all in hopes of sharing similar experiences. Women, who relate to others on the basis of valuing connectedness and intimacy, invite hearing of difficult moments from their loved ones in order to offer their comforting words. What mothers need to watch for are the words of comfort that resemble giving advice or gaining control over their children's lives. Teenage children, both girls and boys, are sensitive to what appears as criticism or judgment of their persons. Tannen especially lifts up this dynamic in the conversation between mothers and daughters. A daughter complains about her difficult day (at school, at work, with husband and children), mother sympathizes with her daughter who, to a mother's great surprise, turns against her, accusing mom of criticism. An innocent remark from Mom, "Oh, honey, you should not have taken on such a load," will sound to her daughter like "You are not capable of multitasking or managing everything yourself." What one side offers as a consolation, the other side takes as judgment and evaluation of one's capabilities. This frequently occurs because we bring to our conversations with people, and particularly with family members, packages of emotions, memories, and misinterpreted messages from past interactions. The other example of misheard communication is this:

Parent asks: "Is Tim [a boyfriend] going to be coming for dinner tomorrow?"

Daughter answers: "Yeah. We're going to be hanging out at the house."

Parent hesitantly: "Tomorrow is not a good time." (In this request there lies no hidden agenda. A parent might simply be feeling tired, not ready for company, or looking forward to a quiet evening.)

Daughter becomes upset: "I knew it. You never liked Tim."

Although the parent did not say that he or she did not like Tim, the daughter hears precisely *that,* because in the past the parent might have showed disapproval. Teenage daughters, who are very much aware of their looks, hairstyles, and clothes, fear a "no" response because they take it as a personal criticism. In the daughter's eye "no" to Tim is a critique of *her* choice. The interaction between fathers and daughters is influenced by tensions similar to those experienced in the relationship with a mother. As a teenage daughter struggles to establish her autonomous self and personal space, she pushes away her parents. While the mother wrestles with her daughter for a close and intimate connection, the father feels more confused if his act of liberty toward his daughter generates more failed communication. For example, a father and his daughter have an argument. The daughter accuses her father of not understanding her, cuts off the conversation, and goes to her room. In her room, she thinks over the conversation, processes her emotions, and *waits* for her dad to come in and talk to her again. Mother would most likely follow up with her daughter after an argument because of females' inherent need to preserve connection and communication. Father, who as a male has a high respect for autonomy, reasons that his daughter appreciates his leaving her alone and honoring her wishes for some personal space. What he does not know is that his daughter perceives his gesture of respect as indifference and abandonment.[31]

Parent-son patterns of communication

While vacationing in my homeland, my husband and I were about to drive my nephew and niece to visit friends. "Put your seat belt on," I told Martin. He did not do anything. I reached toward him and started buckling him up. He became quite agitated. "Don't do it. I know how to do it myself," he said. Any prescriptive language — including the instruction about the seat belt — can release an avalanche of adrenalin and high emotions in boys. Boys' developing masculine identity makes them feel that they do not need to take orders from "girls" because at the core of this feeling is their need to differentiate from mothers and, by extension, from other females. They pretend that they do not need their mothers or caretakers, and this "independence" game further complicates conversations between mothers and their sons. Michael Riera writes, "For many teenagers, searching for identity initially includes buying into the gender stereotypes, especially for boys. As a result, in front of peers they play the male role, staying tough and in charge."[32]

While females relate to one another through talk, males find their common platform for relating through activities, accomplishments, or performances. This mode of relating enables them to demonstrate their individuality by juxtaposing it instead of integrating it with the individualities of others. A son tries to show his father what he can do on his own, how he might be different from his father, or how he might be improving upon and transcending his father's skills and knowledge. He places himself next to his father in hopes of gaining respect and validation of his independent self. Relating to his father is therefore often conditioned by the son's feeling of accomplishment, praise, or encouragement in the process of doing. This dynamic in itself can be a source of destructive communication because it builds upon instructional and prescriptive language that — though not intended to be mentoring or judgmental — can come across as such.

Instructional language can be perceived by teenage children as saying: "You are still a child. You don't know how to do things."[33] Chap and Dee Clark point out that any hints in conversation about what children need to do, what goals they need to accomplish, and what they have not done typically prompt teenage children to give up the conversation with adults.[34] Adolescents' pride and sensitivity to both prescriptive and instructional language shatters regular conversations. Sadly, parents tend to minimize the conversation with their teenage children because it can turn ballistic even when it is about the most innocent of themes. So what to say and how to say things to teenagers?

Emotional swings between being in a great mood and being in a terrible mood that characterize a teenager's personality advise parents to time their words carefully. The Clarks write, "Especially for early adolescents, right after school is one of the worst times to pepper them with questions or try to get them to 'relationally engage.' "[35] When a teenage child is tired, agitated, or down, the best thing is to let conversation go. Communication scholars suggest Internet and social websites as entry points for encouraging teenage children to open up about school, friends, and dilemmas of the adolescent world. "For boys especially," Miriam Weinstein writes, "talking can be easier when they are doing something."[36] Activity time such as sports or manual work and relaxing time (at the computer or at the dinner table) are opportunities to initiate conversation with teenage children. I would not recommend asking broad questions, such as: "How is school?" I would recommend asking a more focused question like: "What sorts of experiments did you do in chemistry class today?" Speaking with my niece about her friends, I learn that to my broad question — "How are your girlfriends?" — she answers, "okay." But when I ask her what the latest fashion her girlfriends wore to school on that particular day, she gives me quite a lengthy answer. This type of conversation is better suited to early adolescents (ten to twelve). Part of the reason is that this age group lingers between concrete thought and entry into formal (abstract thought) processes. Middle adolescents (thirteen to fifteen) and late adolescents (fifteen to eighteen) in particular do not like to comment on chemistry experiments or fashion very much (both of which they consider too trivial for their comment). They like to ask questions about unfairness, cheating, loyalty, or love — more "ethical" issues that they come across in their class or relationships.[37] Loners on the surface, adolescents seek counsel from adults. They do not always ask for it in a straightforward way, and parents are advised to watch for the subtle ways of asking — such as teenager's open door, hanging around the dishwasher as Mom cleans the dishes, or accompanying a parent on a car ride. Michael Riera advises parents: "Deep sharing is not the everyday occurrence between teenagers and parents — at least, not on any kind of consistent basis — [therefore] plan accordingly."[38]

Talking about God with teenagers can occur during both structured and unstructured conversational moments. Having youth reflect on their day at school or probing issues of dating, sports, cliques, grades, or life goals with them around the kitchen table offers families or church groups opportunities for bringing the Christian story to bear on the everyday life issues of a family. Carol Lakey Hess suggests, "Very often, listening to the questions and doubts of young people enables us to share with them important aspects of the faith tradition."[39]

A Window into Family Dinner

How might this play out in the everyday life of a family? Let me offer an example from my own family. During one particular dinnertime, we got into a discussion on fashion with my niece, Daniela. She was talking about the girls in her class who like to exclude other girls based upon the fashion they wear. "If you don't wear the clothes that are in, these girls won't be friends with you," said my niece. Daniela's grandmother asked her: "Is it right to exclude these schoolmates of yours for the clothes they wear? What if their families cannot afford to buy the latest fashion?

You know, such a fashion can be very expensive, right?" Daniela and her grandmother got into a discussion about judging people by outward appearances, differences between privileged and less privileged families, and the issue of who makes for a good friend. Although the grandmother did not bring any particular biblical passage to bear upon the discussion, I saw the conversation as an entry point into engaging a faith perspective. The value this conversation had for spiritual formation is that it helped raise an ethical issue. Further, it challenged the adults and the girl to think about how to respond morally to a real-life situation. This situation pressed for the strategies of nurturing moral reflection, as the issue at stake was the need to develop my niece's capacity for moral response.

In order to nurture moral reflection with youth, adults may try to engage various dilemmas of youth with biblical perspectives. This real-life conversation suggests a possible scenario for how to do it. Parents or other adult caretakers can initiate these conversations by first bringing forward "the news" from the teenager's world. A real-life accident of a New Jersey teenage girl who fell into a manhole in the street while walking and text messaging at the same time might prompt discussion about the intensity of text messaging among teenagers and the value of a face-to-face conversation vis-à-vis a virtual one. Teen-oriented books and magazines also provide parents with real-life situations as conversation starters. For example, a mother goes through the mail and sees that a magazine for teenage girls, *Seventeen*, has arrived. She browses through it and notices and reads an article about hazing at high school sororities. Mom decides to bring the issue up with her daughter, Jessie. Jessie, who attends middle school, complains about her girlfriend who appears to bully her.

Mother: "Jessie, your magazine arrived today in the mail." "Have you had a chance to look at it?"

Jessie: "No, Mom, not yet."

Mother: "There was an article about hazing. I can't believe that this is going on among girls at school. And I did not know that there are sororities at high schools already."

Mom and Jessie can get into discussion about hazing and its ethical implications, with the intention of engaging faith perspectives.

Sometimes adults do not have to involve their teenage children directly when trying to engage youth-situations from a biblical perspective. Discussing real-life issues from a biblical perspective without the direct involvement of their daughter or son, adults cater to a mode of teenage learning that I call overhearing. When asked about her faith perspective, fourteen-year-old Brittney shared with me that she found answers to her dilemmas on her own. "I don't talk to adults when thinking about situations at school or in my life," she told me. Brittney is responsible for her age and enjoys going on mission trips and reading the Bible to senior citizens in assisted living facilities. Although she admits that she does not seek direct advice from adults, she admits that she "overhears" the talk of adults — her parents, her pastor, and others — and draws upon their insights, experiences, and values. Adults' talk about the Bible in particular helps Brittney to form her response to how to live her young life.

Faith formation, as I present it, relies upon helping adolescents to create a narrative identity based in the Bible. This further means that faith formation aims to grow a storied self with adolescents, a storied self by which youth learn to organize their life coherently and infuse it with meaning and purpose. What this identity is, and how families can fashion this identity with their youth is the subject of the next chapter.

You can continue kitchen table youth ministry by:

◆ *Nurturing a narrative identity with your youth*

1. Use family gatherings (such as family reunions, weddings, funerals), religious holidays (Christmas, Easter) or national

holidays (Thanksgiving) to talk with your children about your family narrative. Focus on the themes of roots, journey, family rituals and their meanings, or the personalities of individual family members. The stories told do not have to have God-talk at their center; rather, their purpose is to describe a patterned human activity and to probe youth's imagination to interpret life in relation to faith and divine guidance.

2. Implement various means other than table talk to nurture the growth of the storied self with your youth. Sharing stories over the meal or during its preparation, going through photo albums or scrap books, cleaning out closets, rereading old journals, working together on a project in the workshop, going for drives in the car or going for walks with the dog, all represent opportunities for telling stories.

3. Coach youth into introducing themselves in a way that binds them with a family narrative. This exercise does not necessarily require a specific form of greeting; rather, it coaches youth to adopt a cultural artifact that will give them a sense of family connection. I, for example, admire African American women who intentionally wear particular dresses or fabrics that reflect their families of origin. My friend whose family is of Eastern European origin teaches her daughters how to bake a particular Easter pastry related to the customs of her ancestry. Practicing certain rituals at home (such as a tea ritual), rehearsing or modeling values, using a certain style of conduct are all forms of creating a family narrative. Of course, not every piece of family narrative has a positive influence; values that we teach can restrict rather than expand a youth's horizon. By developing more of a critical ability to interpret family and life patterns of relating and ordering the world, youth will critically scrutinize their family education and, one hopes, hold on to the formatively valuable pieces of it — even if it means learning lessons from negative and stifling examples.

Chapter Four

The Practice of Tilling the Garden

EVERY SATURDAY MORNING Mom bakes a cake to go with our afternoon coffee. She prides herself on her baking skills, and her cakes are always most delicious. Not this recent weekend. The cake felt heavy and dry, and Father and I were wondering what had happened. Mom admitted that she had used a new recipe from a magazine, something she had never done before. "I should not have done it!" she lamented. "The best cakes are the ones from my family cookbook that have already proven their worth." I pulled out an old family cookbook in which were recorded mostly cake recipes. This culinary wisdom had been collected from my grandmother, aunt, cousins, neighbors, Mom's friends, and my brother's and my friends — truly a panoply of baking experiences recorded in a variety of handwriting.

The old book of recipes reminded me of one folk truth: People's identities are formed by the ingredients and different seasonings, and by the kitchen smells and styles of their family. When my parents visited me in the United States, they knew that they were in a strange land because of *the lack* of ingredients that they needed to make a typical Slovak meal. Culinary products from a particular land brand us with distinctive identities. We realize this at the moments we miss our comfort food or, even worse, when we get sick on a new country's diet until our bodies adjust. The recipes in the family cookbook narrate a story grounded in the particular piece of soil, the particular set of agrarian and cooking practices, and in the act of sharing a meal. Such a story can gather families under the umbrella of the shared realization of who they are, where they come from, and what they can create together.

What I call the practice of tilling the garden in this book is the practice of cultivating vocational identity with youth by grounding their experience of life and the self in the story and witness of God's people. Just as we design and cultivate the garden toward a specific purpose (e.g., a vegetable, herb, or flower garden), so we use God's story to cultivate youth's experiences toward their vocation. The practice of tilling the garden of God's story is a practice in which adults instill in youth a vocational language and vocational framework by which youth communicate to themselves and to the world *who* they are and *where* they are heading. It is a practice using metaphors, imagination, and narration through which ididivuals create the story of divine presence in their life and chart the various directions of the call in relation to God's guiding presence.

To cultivate the vocational identity of youth means to cultivate their narrative identity through table talk. This process of telling a story is guided by the biblical narrative that families bring in order to frame their everyday life issues or experiences. Vocational identity, based in the Bible and retold through life narratives, emphasizes telling one's experience in a way that frames it with patterns of God's grace, direction, lesson, purpose, and challenge. It is to this kind of framing and telling of one's life story as one lived in response to God's grace that I invite you.

Vocational Identity and the Contexts of Embodiment

Planting and nurturing youth's understanding of vocation does not happen in a vacuum. It happens among other Christians — specifically one's family — and it happens in a particular place: around the kitchen table. At the kitchen table adults have the opportunity to forge the vocational identity of their family, an identity based on the biblical story of grace, deliverance from sin, and forming a community. Instrumental to this process is a habit of table talk that lays down the ground rules for family conversations. It is through such habits and by such rules that the family stories are told, vocational themes identified, and patterns of divine guidance detected.

Of course, the kitchen table is not the first or only context in which vocational identity is embodied. As Christian believers we have our Christian identities construed and made flesh through the communal life of the body as represented by a faith community, its narrative, sacraments, and practices. For example, the primary work of the Eucharistic sacrament is to form the fellowship or community. In this sacrament young people integrate their identity with the identity of the body of Christ. Luther says, "To receive this sacrament in bread and wine, then, is nothing else than to receive a sure sign of this fellowship and incorporation with Christ and all saints.... If one member suffers, all suffer together; if one member is honored, all rejoice together."[1] The work of sacrament reshapes the spiritual and physical parameters of one's personal identity to include the properties of the whole of Christ's body (from local congregation to the global church, from individual pain to solidarity with hurting others).[2] If we are to share our identity in Christ in its entirety, then this Christian identity formation calls for creating the contexts of embodiment (e.g., spaces, spiritual practices, rhythms of life, actions, etc.). The function of these contexts is to transpose Christ's body into our families, relationships, work places, neighborhoods, and the wider world.

Biblical Context: Garden of Eden

The first embodied context for vocational identity that I want to propose is a biblical metanarrative. From the many available narratives I choose the Yahwist's creation account in Genesis and examine how this narrative tells the story of human vocation. Theologian Sallie McFague observes that "the Genesis myth no longer functions for most people as a working cosmology, as a framework providing a sense of both space and place...possibilities and limitations, for the conduct of daily living."[3] While scientifically speaking neither Genesis creation account yields data compatible with the findings of hard-core science, I would disagree with McFague's claim that the Genesis myth is unable to provide a framework for a person's sense of place or belonging. The Genesis (Yahwist) account of creation is the narrative of the ancient Israelites' way of making sense of their beginning and place in the world. This sense is articulated through their relationship to soil, farming, and tilling the land. The vocational identity of this ancient nation emerges out of its experience of interrelatedness and interdependence on the soil, rain, sunshine, farm animals, community, the patriarchs, and Yahweh.

The Israelites' narrative experience describes vocation in terms of a divine act of creating, care, and formation. In the biblical garden we see the prototype of divine vocation: God is a potter when God forms a man from the dust; God is a gardener when God plants the garden and the trees. God's role is to create, guide, and sustain. God sees to it that Adam and Eve have a plentitude of resources, such as fauna and flora, that provide them with food, company, pleasure, work, activity, and rest for mind and body. According to the Genesis account, God the Creator does not interfere with Adam and Eve's life in the garden; the explicit instruction God gives Adam is that he may eat the fruit from all the trees in the garden except the tree of the knowledge of good and evil. Disobeying God's command will result in death.

The first human vocation is narrated in terms of delegating tasks to a man and a woman. The task to till and keep the garden is invested with a purpose for human beings' existence in the garden. This purpose involves creativity (such as giving names to all the species created by God), industry, maintaining life, and learning to live within the ecology of other living organisms. The values and skills implicit in this task define the fundamental characteristics of human life: work and communion with others.

This task is not discontinued after the Fall; rather it is infused with the new dimensions of being (e.g., pain, struggle to survive, struggle for intimacy, etc.).[4] After the man and the woman disobey God's command, God pronounces a verdict:

> To the woman he said, "I will greatly increase your pangs in childbearing; in pain you shall bring forth children, yet your desire shall be for your husband, and he shall rule over you." (Gen. 3:16; NRSV)

Feminists bracket these verses as sexist, as a basis for oppressing and demeaning women.[5] But if we look at and interpret Genesis 3:16 and Genesis 3:17–19 through historical, narrative, and human development lenses, these verses tell of the experiences of people in a particular time and place. The writer of the Yahwist account (known as J) is praised for "his insight into human nature and the recognition that a higher order and purpose may lie behind seemingly incomprehensible human events."[6] I hold that these experiences express nonscientific observations of the cultural and general developmental tendencies for women's and men's physical and psycho-social growth.[7]

The narrative of Genesis 3:16 is a product of Israel's ninth-century B.C.E. patriarchal culture. Woman's childbearing role and submissiveness to her husband are described by this culture as the workings of a woman's inner predisposition for love and connectedness. Different societies in different centuries renegotiate these roles in order to find fresh personal and cultural expressions for female intimacy in addition to these more traditional ones. The desire for her husband to which God "predestines" the woman implies both her desire to live in a community and her ability to give birth to and nurture communality. This narrative tells us that a woman's destiny is marked by her capacity for communion, relationship, intimacy, and nurture. The sense of woman's existential trajectory points to the very fabric of her being — woven from the fibers of relationality, companionship, connectedness, and intimacy.

The verdict for the man is the following:

And to the man he said, "Because you have listened to the voice of your wife, and have eaten of the tree about which I commanded you, 'You shall not eat of it,' cursed is the ground because of you; in toil you shall eat of it all the days of your life; thorns and thistles it shall bring forth for you; and you shall eat the plants of the field. By the sweat of your face you shall eat bread until you return to the ground, for out of it you were taken; you are dust, and to dust you shall return." (Gen. 3:17–19; NRSV)

The punishment that God articulates for man reflects the reality of the lost blessing. Man, as God's first human creation, lost his special status, and his disobedience made God curse the earth out of which man was formed. The earth with the products it yields will continue to keep the man alive, yet its embedded curse turns against the man in the form of challenges, obstacles, and barriers in his life. The destiny of the man is now to wrestle with the earth, with the same material from which he was created, in order to ensure survival. Wrestling with the earth results in a pioneering spirit in the name of which the man engages in territorial conquests, exploration, and taming and cultivating the land and the sea. Man's existential destiny plays out as a relationship between the very material of his existence (soil) and his urge to dominate, control, and work on this life-giving soil.

A developmental lens helps illuminate different behavioral trajectories to which God "predestines" the woman and the man. However, human developmental tendencies are not the primary embodied contexts for vocational identity. In other words, the way in which we develop does not constitute our vocational identity. The primary source for vocational identity is the creating work of God. Both the man and the woman need to understand their vocational identities in relation to who they are: God's own life breath.[8] At the heart of man and woman's being lies their connectedness and unity with their Creator. This initial unity with the divine is broken by their act of disobedience, which infests their core with uncleanness that is decidedly unacceptable to the holiness and purity of divine being. Staining the ground that they shared with their Creator, Adam and Eve have to leave the garden. Vocation then carries an aspect of judgment, which God announces when the man and the woman disobey him. Equally vocation carries the aspect of love, which is the breath of God in human beings.

God the Creator plowed the human soul with a furrow between being (who one is) and existing (what one needs to do for one's survival). This generative conflict manifests itself as a destiny to create "I–agency" (through work, industry, creativity, production, survival) and to define one's very fabric of being (connectedness with God, roots, being part of, location). When we have a vocation, on one hand, our destiny is to create a sense of personal agency and legacy through work, creativity, production, and industry. On the other hand, we seek to restore and define our connectedness with our Creator through loving, planting roots, nurturing communities, and looking for a place to belong. Human vocation is always embodied. First, it is embodied in the soil from which we came; second, it is embodied in the breath of divine Spirit; and third, it is embodied in communities. Soil connects us with our Creator; the breath of divine Spirit gives us life and sends us forth as autonomous, creative, and unique human beings; and communities create spaces and practices for our vocations. Wherever we go, we start from a place — from a place of creation, love, and grace; whatever we do, we do it under the guidance of the Holy Spirit and encircled by our mentoring communities. Discerning our vocational identity means recognizing that we are the children of God first, and that we need to respond to whatever task our Trinitarian God calls us. We discern our vocations through heart (that is, the level of our intimate connection with God), through mind (that is, the level of our personal agency), and through body (that is, the level of life that was breathed in us through divine Spirit). Faith and trust in the Trinitarian God, personal agency, and our individual uniqueness give shape to our vocations.

In the Eucharist we participate in yet another part of divine vocation — one that precedes all human vocational strivings and that is embodied in the body and blood of Jesus Christ. Because of Christ's own vocation, manifested through his redeeming death on the cross, we do not need to use our vocation to gain salvation. The door to the garden has been opened by the love and grace of our God in Christ. In the Eucharist, we are invited to experience God's nourishment and sustenance, which recalls the promise of nourishment from the biblical garden. In the Eucharist we taste the feast of the trees from the garden again because we have been reconciled to God through Christ. What we seek through our vocation is then a way to respond, to honor the gift of life our Trinitarian God gave us through the soil, through God's breath, and through God's Son Jesus Christ.

Developmental Context: Generativity

Existential reflection on the biblical narrative of creation suggests that human beings are defined by love and by work. This notion has been developed by great theorists of the human condition: Freud, Erikson, and others propose that the anxiety of human life stems from the need for industry and the need for intimacy. Vocation, conceived developmentally, reflects this inner drive of humans for work and love. In the language of human development, this inner drive is called generativity. Developed by Eric Erikson, the concept joins industry and intimacy into a felt desire of human beings to give birth to children, to create new ideas, and to manufacture new things in order to ensure continuity of life, creation, and the self. The same concept also refers to felt parental responsibility to take care of the next generation and provide for its physical, mental, emotional, and spiritual needs. As generative adults, people act on their inner desire for agency and communion.[9]

Psychologists describe agency as a way to extend oneself beyond mortality, meaning that individuals' fear of death motivates them to create personal, vocational, or ideological legacies that can be passed on to the next generation. Forming agency thus represents an approach enabling the self to exert power, build autonomy, and fashion values by which the self will be distinguished and preserved in the life cycle of its own family or society. A person's desire for communion expresses the need to live in relationships with others, provide care, nurture, and love to others, and to receive a degree of it back. Unlike agency, this desire does not necessarily center on the need for power and conquering the world. Rather, it builds on the need to be needed by others as a parent, provider, protector, guarantor, mentor, guide, teacher, and so forth.

The inner drive of agency focuses on crafting and developing persons in relation to their individualized skills, potential, and ambition. The inner drive of communion orients a person toward an integrated life in a community, redirecting the ambitions of the self to bear on the life of the unit (be it a biological family, church, or nation). Generativity that is fueled by agency yields different fruits than the generativity motivated by communion. Occupational or professional fulfillment, intellectual or artistic achievement, civic and church involvement are expressions of generative behavior based in agency. Parenting, fostering, and mentoring children are expressions of generative behavior based in communion. The generative behavior of an adult is ideally driven by both agency and communion, yet the relationship between these two drives tends to be unbalanced. Focus on agency makes generative people emphasize work and productivity at the expense of relationships. Focus on communion has generative people dwell on the importance of relationships with others, sometimes to the degree that a person's own needs and autonomy remain underdeveloped.[10]

Generativity and Adolescence

Erikson linked generativity to a particular life stage (middle adult years) and articulated it as a property of the individual. The question is whether the task of generativity can be applied to different stages of life (e.g., adolescence) or to a group of people such as family or nation. And if it could be so applied, what would it mean? Researchers suggest that "generativity is not a discrete stage in human development but follows its own course based on cultural roles and life circumstances."[11] Although generative behavior culminates in middle adulthood (thirty-five to forty-two), generative tendencies can be cultivated beginning in childhood, and they appear to be conditioned culturally as much as developmentally.

Erikson coined the term "generativity" to indicate the direction in which sexual energy (genitality) of adult people is channeled. It is channeled, he says, through a wish to combine their personalities and energies in the production and care of common offspring.[12] Passing on one's genetic capital through giving birth to babies is one aspect of the complex concept, and as Erikson states, "[it] does not itself attest to generativity."[13] Additional aspects include intention and preparedness to take care of children physically and nurture them emotionally, spiritually, and mentally.

The stage of adolescent development focuses on the task of developing a personal identity, and it is preoccupied with a meaningful construction of a belief system, social roles, sexuality, and vocational sense. Granted a "moratorium" in life by adults (another Eriksonian term), a youth has time for making transitions from the life of a child to the life of an adult member of society. This is a time of experimentation and figuring out ways to meet societal expectations that can range from respectable attire, vocational choices, partner choices, spiritual choices — all in the name of successful integration into the broader society. Adolescents many times come across as a distinct tribe because they are working out their integration through separation and distancing themselves from the social contracts agreed upon by the adult members of society. Rejection or challenging of these contracts is an adolescent way of testing their validity, purposefulness, and usefulness for defining membership in the community of human beings.

This challenge on the part of adolescence is more than their constant praxis of provocation (although it may seem to be only that to the exhausted parents of adolescents). Adolescents desire to stretch the world around them, acting consciously or subconsciously on their drive to construct meaning. They grow in their potential to rewrite and re-create the norms of the adult world. Through experimentation and critique, adolescents unmask its inconsistencies, flaws, and hypocrisies. As a result of their idealism, the adolescents are able to generate a tension between the status quo or torpor on the one hand and vitality and agency of communities on the other. I do not suggest that generativity as a biological concept that encourages procreation be applied to adolescents (although we have teen pregnancies and teen parents, and we will continue to have biologically generative young people regardless). But is there a potential for the application of generativity to adolescence in its cultural sense?

As a cultural term, generativity implies different sets of expectations from society to society. Psychologist Dan McAdams writes, "We expect men and women in their 40s to be generative in some way. By contrast, we expect less by way of generativity from young people."[14] Protected by this moratorium, youth in industrialized societies of the twenty-first century tend to be deliberately dissuaded from taking on work, decision-making responsibilities, or executive roles. In more traditional agrarian societies, youth are incorporated more quickly as adult members of communities, having tasks delegated to them that require both physical and mental care of their community. Christian educator David White points out that "the social institution of adolescence, like Frankenstein's monster, is not natural."[15] He goes on to explain the disruptive impact that can occur when society tries to contain the creative energies and, I would add, prophetic voices, of its youth through a culturally defined understanding of adolescence. Cultural generativity of youth is manifested through their "shaping a better world, including roles in every major peace and justice, labor, civil rights, and environmental movement in modern history — and the various contemporary antiwar, anti-sweatshop and antiglobalization movements."[16]

When applied to the stage of adolescence, generativity as a cultural term lifts up youth's proclivity to reconstruct the world as they search for meaning and imagine fresh alternatives. Cultural generativity of youth is developmentally encouraged by their growth of mental and physical capabilities. Every culture seeks to incorporate youth successfully into its system of values, traditions, relationships, and work force. Raising a rebellious, vagrant youth, without a sense of direction or life meaning, is like building a bridge to self-destruction for any society. What adolescence as a social construct should perhaps provide is the creation of purposeful direction for youth. In other words, giving youth a time to transition from childhood to adulthood is also giving time and opportunity to adults as parents, caretakers, guardians, etc., to orient the generative tendencies of youth toward a constructive and positive direction.

Generativity and Family

In their essay on family generativity, Dollahite, Slife, and Hawkins expand the understanding of generativity from a trait on inner drive to a set of generative connections. What is seen as an evolutionary drive when it comes to nurturing the young is redefined by the advocates of family generativity in a more holistic manner to emphasize "human agency over the functioning of internal drives and response to cultural pressures."[17] In other words, taking care of one's family is a matter of choice and moral responsibility rather than biological function. In order to sustain care, a family develops and draws on the values that bind individual family members into commitments and practices of nurture. When the language of generativity emphasizes family agency as opposed to individual agency, it helps integrate an individual's efforts for creativity and the birthing of people, things, or ideas into the broader narrative of cosmic striving. This metanarrative concerns itself with life and its preservation and continuity across time, culture, and space. Being part of this metanarrative orients individuals toward considering the moral impact and accountability of their agency. In other words, knowing that my agency is part of the divine design of things, I not only follow a certain direction, but I also reflect on how my generative actions might shape and influence the other parts of God's design.

One of the tensions that parents experience occurs when they decide to execute their parenting efforts individualistically. Let's say that a father believes in a laissez-faire style of parenting and a mother prefers to give more direction and instruction to her children. Clinging stubbornly to two different parenting philosophies confuses children and lets them slip through the cracks of their parents' own inability to find a compromise. Conceiving generativity holistically, i.e., as an agency that is shared and shaped by family, can yield practices of care and nurture that preserve continuity of time (e.g., between generations of parents, grandparents, and children), of values, and space. When a family dislocates from the primary network of care (maternal and paternal grandparents, aunts, uncles, cousins), as often occurs when parents divorce, or one of the parents dies or a family moves because of job pressures, the result is the loss of care and nurture as a shared family practice. Nurture and care can become a highly individualized process in which the children can experience a one-sided, narrow direction from a parent, stripped of the connections and continuity with a broader family narrative. Family generativity hopes to transcend selfishness and an understanding of parenting generativity as the extension and realization of the individual self. Family generativity respects individual agency as it relates to and cooperates with the family network.

Narrative Context: Divine Metaphors in Human Life

Passing on the faith to young people involves helping them to create a narrative identity guided by a vocational framework. This means teaching them how to see and narrate their lives within the framework of God's story of grace, guidance, and faithfulness. This process begins in the context of generative behavior, first, by youth, who engage their curiosity, agency, and the exploration of the world; and second, by adults, who commit to taking care of their offspring in a spiritually formative way. The adults commit to provide material resources, but they also commit to intentionally interpreting life experiences and stories of their teenagers through a faith perspective.

Formation of identity, whether personal, religious, or vocational, is the central task of adolescence. Striving to understand oneself in relation to a panoply of questions of both cosmic and practical significance needs an organizing principle. Narrative psychology suggests that it is through narrative identity that a person binds the multitude of life choices and prospects into a coherent whole. The randomness of life with its runaway patterns of meaning can begin to make sense if captured through a story. Psychologist Dan McAdams describes narrative identity this way: "Narrative identity links together episodic memories and future goals to define an adult life in time and social context."[18]

Narrative identity begins to take shape in adolescent years, in the phase of identity formation. In the search for a system of belief and ethics the adolescents have an opportunity to construe a narrative identity that provides a way of talking about one's life and offers a narrative compass by which to navigate through life's complexities. The ability to form narrative identity in adolescents begins with the onset of formal operations (abstract thought). Adolescents begin to develop their narrative identities through keeping journals or writing stories. These represent "rough drafts" of fully developed narrative identity that occurs in adulthood.[19] In terms of spiritual formation, adults need to seize the opening for patterning their youth's identity into a storied self. Young people who begin to learn how to order their lives into a redemptive narrative also begin to understand the framework of hope that orients life toward generative behavior. As much as generativity is an activity, it also represents a way of thinking about and narrating one's life.[20]

Metaphors of Redemption:
A Christian Perspective

Narrating their lives through metaphors of redemption, generative people express their belief in the power of redemption, the source of which can be transcendence (religion) or the redemptive self in its sociocultural context (individual in relation to economic, educational, parenting, or health challenges). For Christians the paradigm of redemption has its source in being graciously forgiven by our God in Jesus Christ. Luther explained redemption by the concept of justification by grace through faith. The doctrine of justification was Luther's reaction against the scholastic theology of the medieval Roman Catholic Church. The Roman Catholic Church allowed the notion that individuals are able to gain their salvation by accumulation of merits for their good works. Luther's reply was that one is saved by the *action* of God as manifested in the death and resurrection of Jesus Christ. The fruits of God's redeeming action in Jesus Christ are further explicated through the language of vocation. One's relationship to God and God's creation changes under God's justifying action. This further means that a heart that has been justified leads a person to a response that finds its expression in the service to one's neighbor. A person's vocation in the world is firmly based in a call to the Gospel and in faith in Jesus Christ. This call empowers the individual believers to see their lives as the bearers of good fruit that will benefit the world around them. The theological nature of vocation expresses itself as an activity and attitude by which believers are moved to praise, to serve, and to co-create with God after being given the promise of eternal salvation in Jesus Christ.

Vocation renders the relationship between one's faith and engagement with society to be participatory in God's love, preservation, and care for God's Kingdom.

Imagining my Vocation

Vocation provides a redemptive theme around which a youth can weave a narrative identity. It is a narrative that emphasizes human life as an individual's response to God's grace bestowed at baptism. To form a youth's vocational identity through a narrative, adults can draw on the power of this story to nurture a youth's imagination and active consciousness. Vocation comes from God in Christ, who calls an individual to follow God's paths. Since these paths are not clearly demarcated, vocation then builds on the faculty of imagination. Discerning God's call very much depends on an individual's ability to imagine herself in the realm of new personal, family, and social reconfigurations. The role of imagination is to help people to envision themselves in the positions that calling might demand.

What family narratives influenced my sense of vocational identity? As a child I would listen to the stories of the adult members of my family, and I would learn that my family had a history of intellectual leadership and pastoral service in the community. This family narrative offered direction for my personal storyline. My vocational identity, shaped by my family's stories, evolved around the issues of justice, leadership, and emancipation. My sense of vocation (not career) involves an urge to be an advocate for women's rights in family, university, and workplace; to restore justice to those who were oppressed and suffered unjustly because of their faith convictions under communism, and to educate families and their children in the faith tradition. To pursue my vocation, I had to fight strong patriarchal traditions in the Slovak culture and the church, and to change careers in order to find the most natural setting for my vocation. Imagination came in handy in my vocational struggle because it empowered me to surrender my secular career in Slovakia for studying theology in the United States. As author Dori Baker says, "Transforming a tradition laden with a patriarchal bias requires new metaphors."[21]

Through their family narrative, children, youth, and even adults become familiar with the themes, values, and approaches to personal empowerment that help trigger their sense of vocation in life. These stories may lie dormant in a person for a long time; however, their value is not in how quickly they can affect a person's life; rather, their value is in their being treasure chests of memory, tradition, wisdom, and life experience. What becomes of us depends on our ability to imagine how the stories of our tradition play out in the stories of our future possibilities. Imagination releases the mind from the bondage of habitual thinking and thought patterns. It provides wings to fly across boundaries of gender, race, class, or geography. Maxine Greene, who writes about the interrelatedness of imagination and social consciousness, points to the fact that imagination itself does not change social realities such as economic or political oppression. That takes structural societal means such as legislation, executive decisions, or civic infrastructure. The role of imagination, Greene writes, "is to awaken, to disclose the ordinarily unseen, unheard, and unexpected."[22] The role of active consciousness is to provide a form to the alternatives awakened by the act of imagining.

Imagining Vocation through Bible

In reframing the discussion of imagination and social consciousness through reading biblical stories, the subject of discussion becomes that of a center. The loss of center awakens imagination, and the alternatives that imagination sprouts forth give form to social consciousness. Losing the center implies the surrender of safe, comfortable ways of thinking; such surrender occurs when individuals lose stability in their lives (loss of a member of one's family, loss of health, a place to live, or income). By centering our lives on routines and stereotypical thinking, we grow into predictable believers, but not imaginative believers. We strengthen our abilities to adhere to the old, but we weaken our responsiveness to Christ-filled vocation and discipleship. Biblical stories narrate a movement of decentering characters' lives from the zone of safety, familiarity, or the ordinary to the zone of ambiguity, the undefined, and the gray. The examples of the story of Adam and Eve, Job, Ruth and Noami, Moses and Jesus' disciples in Acts all witness to a loss of center. The loss of center is the loss of home (paradise), trust (relationship between God the Creator and Adam and Eve), status and health (Job), favorable living conditions (famine and death of family providers in Ruth), death of their beloved Teacher and dispersion of his early followers (Christ's disciples and the destruction of their early community in Jerusalem). The lives of the characters in these and other stories have been influenced by God's judging, redeeming, and transforming action. It is not until the characters see their lives imaginatively, through faith, through new calling and mandates, that they are able to participate fully in the reality of redemption.

Through imagination youth can intuit the calling from God by which they are delegated to embark on a distinctive journey. The process of developing vocational identity requires that youth construe their stories in an imaginative way. The imaginative construal of youth's lives is an exercise in narrating their life using redemptive patterns. The guiding metaphor of redemption is that God in Christ is the One who imagines a person's paths, molds them, and bequeaths meanings to that person's life. Narrative identity is a metastory through which adults coach youth to voice-over the cultural narrative of individualistic success and survival with the redemptive story of vocation. Such a metastory helps liberate youth from the sociocultural pressures of their lives. Such biblical stories offer youth images and metaphors for surrendering their cultural selves in order to imagine their destiny with God in Christ. That is to say, vocation is not anybody's private vocation; one shares it with the characters in the scriptural narratives.

How to imagine a personal story of vocation

When developing narrative identity with youth, I have two objectives in mind: first, to stir the imagination of youth by asking them to reflect on the metaphors in which God in Christ shows his presence in their lives and can be the source of their vocational identities; and second, to stir the imagination of youth by asking them to discern divine metaphors and events that shape the vocational identities of biblical characters. The two objectives build one another up in that the second objective provides the interpretative lens for viewing the first objective. And the first objective builds the bridge to biblical stories by creating the common platform (human experience) for shared themes of meaning, purpose, or struggle.

With regard to the first objective, reflection on young people's own narratives needs to be incorporated into a family's narrative. Why? Because youth do not own a rich enough repertoire of life stories at their age. The burgeoning growth of their storied selves is strengthened by the stories of their families, and by literature or art. The family can employ various concrete means to nurture the growth of the storied self with their youth. Sharing stories over a meal or recipe, going through family photo albums or scrapbooks, emptying wardrobes or attics, rereading old journals, working in the shed or workshop with tools, recreational activities: all these are opportunities for telling stories or passing on to youth values and attitudes. When developing a narrative vocational identity with youth through their and their family's life narratives, it is important to identify themes or occurrences that are generative. It is not the fact that these events themselves carry omens of calling or special destiny; rather, they prompt the imagination to interpret and narrate them. Human life cannot be narrated without making a reference to God's involvement in it. There is *no* human story in which a question regarding God would not be involved.

When searching for metaphors of the divine, I do not insist that adults push youth into always seeing divine presence in either biblical or personal stories. Stories need to account for a tension between God's revealing presence in Jesus Christ and God's mysterious hiddenness. There are stories in which God is hidden, silent, and invisible to the eyes of faith. There are typically stories in which one sees what is evil but not what is divine. Our experience of the void is as real as our experience of the holy. The story of the redemptive self is also the story of the unfeasibility of redeeming every tragic moment of human life.[23]

My second objective in reading Bible stories with youth relies on family as well as on congregational leadership. The second objective places its focus on the biblical story as a metastory that interprets life through the redemptive lens and as such reverses habitual patterns of thinking or living. As a training and interpretative text, biblical story offers examples of the development of vocational identity. Let me use Moses' story, the part that narrates Moses' call, and suggest the kind of questions that can prompt vocational imagination with youth. His is a story of a leader to whom God delegated a historical task of leading the Israelites out of Egypt. Born to a Jewish woman in Egypt, Moses followed the path of a special destiny: he was able to survive the pharaoh's threat due to his mother's determination to save her son's life, the danger of drowning when floating in the basket on the Nile river, and escaping punishment for killing an Egyptian. In real life, one could name these three incidents as evidence of luck on Moses' part. One could also interpret them as metaphors of divine intervention, the purpose of which will be revealed later in the story. The story does not reveal much regarding how Moses was groomed for his special task. Growing up in the pharaoh's court might have been an advantage because it equipped Moses with a familiarity of courtly society and its mores. Or seeing how his people were mistreated might have created compassion for their fate. Had Moses reflected on his life and experiences in Egypt, he might have been able to identify generative events leading to his vocation.

After Moses had fled from Egypt, he plunged into a life of routines: he became a husband, a father, and he tended a flock of sheep. Upheaval of his previous life turned into bucolic rhythms of care for family and cattle. It is at this stage of Moses' life that God intervenes explicitly through a burning bush. Metaphorically speaking, Moses' life catches on fire when the mandate from God requires that he burn his old routines and lifestyle. Moses' life can be viewed as a manifestation of God's companionship from the very beginning or as a string of lucky coincidences.

The skill of vocational imagination regarding Moses' call can be probed by questions such as these: How does God enter Moses' story and call Moses to his special task? What are the images of God's intervention? What are the ways in which the character shifts the focus from his or her life to God's call? Does Moses lack imagination when he at first says no to his new calling from God? These questions can train young people's minds and eyes to see the clues of divine presence and guidance in their life. These are not necessarily the questions that will provide an instant answer to the question of "What am I supposed to do with my life?" Rather, they suggest to youth what to ask about life.

The next part of the exercise is to focus on the narrative identity of Moses himself. How does Moses narrate his life? The little we know about this is recorded in the conversation between Moses and God: Moses struggles with his mandate. He tries to persuade God that he is not equipped for the task. He does not seem to structure his life, at least initially, around God's call. Moses' narrative identity points to the themes of self-doubt, the awareness of his speech impediment, comfort with his everyday life, and the fear of the task. Such narrative identity is very human, and it can be close to a youth's heart. Struggles with confidence, insecurity, or realization of one's gifts are perennial themes of adolescent life. But does God change Moses' narrative? How? What does God do? Inviting youth to write a narrative identity of biblical characters is like writing a story about a story.

When developing narrative identities of biblical characters, youth are tutored to create commentaries on their own life stories. They are coached into reflecting on divine patterns of care, intervention, silence, and empowerment. We know how some of the biblical stories end. In a youth's story the end and the life alternatives have to be imagined and constantly negotiated with fluid life circumstances. The significance of this exercise is that it emphasizes that we are part of the shared heritage of struggle for vocation that God guides in God's mysterious ways.

The Case of Brittney[24]

Fourteen-year-old Brittney is a bright, sensitive, and fun-loving teenager. As we chat together in her house and I inquire about school, she goes and gets a school project for my husband and me to read. Her way of thinking about her young life commands my admiration: it is full of steadfast perseverance and determination to wrestle with the personal challenges posed to her and her family. One of the challenges that Brittney writes about is her parents' divorce and move. Brittney narrates these experiences with the following words:

> When I was about four years old, my parents got divorced. It was kind of hard for me to handle it back then, but I've adjusted pretty well. Some people would think that your parents getting divorced would change a kid a lot, but I really don't think I would be any different if they were still married. It is hard to make this kind of thing seem positive at all, but to look at the bright side, at least it happened when I was really young and didn't really know what was going on.

Brittney's mother is the sole caretaker of her and her younger sister. They moved to a new neighborhood in which Brittney and her sister started from scratch in terms of finding new friends, and building their reputation and alliances in a new school system. Brittney writes the following about this experience:

In October of 2003, I moved from [the city] to a suburb. I think this changed me a lot because if I hadn't moved here I would have different friends, and I would have grown up in a different neighborhood where the schools are a lot worse than they are here. I could have made this into a really sad event in my life, but instead I looked at the positive parts of it. If I had stayed there I might have met some bad kids or had to move when I was older and already made some really strong friendships with the people there.

Her short narratives captured my attention because they convey hope, a positive outlook, and determination. Brittney's emerging narrative identity shows the themes of personal empowerment. When I talk to her about the sources of her empowerment (e.g., church, youth groups, conversation with adults), she tells me that she does not talk to adults directly about her experiences, but she listens to the adult talk, to the message she gets in her youth group or in the church. Brittney's experiences with the youth group and the mission trips seem to shape her positive self-understanding:

I am very proud of myself for being a kind person and helping people. When I was on the mission trip we helped a lot of people. I also go to nursing homes with my church and talk to the elderly people. Me and the rest of the girls will talk to the old women and paint their nails or they will tell us about their lives. We also volunteer at Salvation Army a lot. The summer between ninth and tenth grade I might be going to Alaska to do missionary work there and help work on houses that have been damaged or need fixing.

The act of "overhearing" the messages of the Gospel, her mother, grandmother, and other adults in her life subtly forms the way in which Brittney thinks and narrates her experiences.

Reflecting on Brittney's case, I would say that forming narrative identity with youth means providing them with the message that can shape their sense of self toward hope and a call to life that is vocational — lived in the imagination and trust of God's sovereignty and purpose for their lives. Narrative vocational identity involves the process of interpreting one's life alongside the themes of divine guidance, intention, and metaphorical presence of God. It calls for an act of imagination and narration. It calls for cooperation between the church's instruction and family conversation. Above all, it calls for the faithful presence of adults in the lives of youth. It is to this theme that I turn in the next chapter.

You can continue kitchen table youth ministry by:

◆ *Using culinary experience to tell the story of your roots*

I encourage families to use their culinary experience (preparing meals, using special ingredients, serving the meals) as teaching tools. What do family recipes, particular ingredients, even cooking dishes tell you about your roots? Evaluate family meals vis-à-vis fast food restaurants in their ability to convey to your family a sense of geographical groundedness. Many local or ethnic restaurants carry regional or national themes; can you re-create a similar thematic pertaining to your family history and story through your family meals? You do not have to do this every night; you might start with holidays or family markers important to your family such as birthdays and anniversaries.

◆ *Using your dining experience wisely*

Use meals to talk about individual family members. What in their life stories do you consider inspirational, courageous, providential; or what you do perceive as lost opportunity, tragic, or unrealized? Are you able to tell the story about your family and the accompanying themes of their lives? Where does your family narrative break? How much of the family narrative are your teenage children able to tell? I am surprised at how many times families use their time together unwisely. Getting together for Thanksgiving might be one of those precious occasions, and it is quite frivolous to spend the family time by watching TV or only in small talk. Be wise stewards of your family time.

◆ *Writing a commentary on the lives of biblical characters*

This exercise is more suited to congregations and their youth groups. Choose a biblical story from the Old or New Testament. Ask your youth to write a commentary on it, focusing on themes of calling and divine guidance. How do they see or not see God calling or guiding the characters in the story? Train young people's eyes to see patterns of God's activity in the story, and then ask them to apply the same approach to their lives. What are the metaphors or courses of action through which they can detect God's presence and guidance? What are the instances in which they do not see God? With which struggles and journeys of the Biblical characters can they identify?

This is quite a mature exercise and is better suited to middle and late adolescents. Do it over the course of time. View this exercise more as a method, and as you invite youth to share the events of their day or week introduce them to this tool of writing a commentary.

Chapter Five

The Practice of Sharing Commons

G ROWING UP IN FORMER COMMUNIST CZECHOSLOVAKIA meant that as a child I participated in various age-based ideological organizations. My participation included celebrating particular rites of passage. For example, to mark my becoming a "young pioneer" in third grade, I wore a blue shirt that my teacher ritually adorned by tying a bright red scarf around my neck. I remember gathering in the city square in front of the imposing bronze bust of Russian revolutionary Vladimir I. Lenin, while being encouraged by our teachers to remain still and reverent for the ceremony. I remember also the mandatory procession on May 1, the International Day of Labor, labor representing one of the core values of communist ideology. On this day, the entire population of the city's schools, factories, and other institutions marched through the city's main street, waving flags and other props in front of the podium on which the communist party officials stood. The march represented a staged gesture of the people's alliance with the party and its values.

As I reflect on these images now, I recall enjoying seeing the city's population come together in a public manner to commemorate May 1, but perhaps more so to embody and enjoy the underlying themes of May 1, themes such as camaraderie — through festive activities that included music, drinks, balloons, and cotton candy — and often also to celebrate sunshine and warm weather. Beneath the superficial homogeneity that the communist regime imposed upon us in the former Czechoslovakia, a person could find an intriguing diversity of individual narratives, ethnic origins, ideologies, confessional beliefs, etc. I particularly liked what I call in this chapter the act of *sharing commons* — though for me the value and contribution of these gatherings to human community was stymied by the ideological underpinnings.

When people come together to share commons, they overtly or openly negotiate patterns of human interaction and discourse. In our communist-style apartment, I observed how people learned to live in tight quarters with one another. Take, for example, the schedule of after hours quiet time (usually running from ten in the evening to six in the morning) during which the tenants were not supposed to make loud noise. The rules about this were posted at the entrance to each building, and for the most part they were respected. People whose lives rubbed up against each other closely used the shared space to forge a paradigm of living that attempted to be dignified for all. As in every community there were of course transgressors of the "apartment complex law," usurpers of common space, and rebels against communal life, but this did not stop the organizing efforts of the community to create the platform for recognizing mutual needs.

In a way, one's intrusion into another person's space and life became inevitable in an apartment complex. Negatively, this style of living infringed upon a person's or a family's privacy; positively, it created everyday opportunities for people to cross paths and engage in conversation and other exchange. By contrast, the current architectural and life styles of contemporary U.S. society tend to segregate its population into suburbia, inner-city, gated communities, etc., using railroad-crossing or bridges to draw lines between neighborhoods and thus between people themselves. The practice of sharing commons is a way of overcoming this human fragmentation, for sharing in one another's humanity means seeing, interacting, and crossing paths with those who have backgrounds and stories different from our own.

Sharing Commons:
Crossing Paths for the Sake of a Better Good

Our discussion of generativity in the previous chapter suggested that human beings are interconnected in their inner drive to help and to be helped. As generative human beings we have different needs, but we also have the need to express our gifts in order to meet each other's needs. Sharing commons means sharing space and interaction, and this cultivates people's sense of contributing to and being part of human community and discourse. Of course people come together all the time: at stadiums to watch sports events, in fields to attend concerts or movies, over barbecues and drinks, and so forth. How does the kind of interaction that people experience in a field or a sports arena differ from the interaction that occurs in sharing commons?

Sharon Daloz Parks suggests that the act of sharing commons invests in people a sense of shared life and of contributing to a common good.[1] The practice of sharing commons builds upon the fact that regardless of their age members of the human family have their different personalities, qualities, and energies through which they can shape the world for better or worse. Sharing commons directs the flow of human energy positively and constructively by using the power of space, practices, and human interaction guided by the biblical narrative. Applying to youth this prac- tice of sharing commons raises the following kinds of questions: Where do young people's lives intersect with the lives of others? Where do they encounter the neighbor, the one who is different, or older or younger, the stranger or the friend? Where do youth hear and respond to other people's stories? What practices guide that interaction? What narrative guides the interaction? When youth share commons, they have a unique opportunity to expand their understanding of the breadth, complexity, and richness of humanity. They are not limited to sharing commons with only their families, for they can share virtual commons, cross-cultural commons (at schools or by traveling), or cross-denominational commons. Sharon Daloz Parks observes: "Travel, communications, and entertainment technologies, along with the emergence of a global market and growing awareness of our interdependence within the natural environment, have cast us all into a new global commons."[2] But precisely because youth have the freedom to grow as global citizens and encounter different, new, exciting, or puzzling features of human community, of course significant risks exist as well. In order to be able to navigate through the variety of commons, youth need to be equipped with an understanding of the heart of community, the patterns of relating, and the unifying narrative.

Throughout this book I have argued for the creation of the physical space and practices such as sharing a meal and conversation. The kitchen table, I suggested, acts as a physical space that embodies and initiates its members into community by manifesting its tangibles (e.g., care, nourishment, physical presence, postures, emotions, attitudes). This space is a basic one in which children can learn the rules of conversation and practice them, or develop their family's sense of ethnic identity through means such as having particular meals prepared with certain ingredients, learning table etiquette, etc. The process of recognizing what the different generations can bring to the table can also start at the table. For example, when we visit a grandmother who bakes a delicious apple pie for her family, we are quick to praise her baking skills. Saying "That was delicious," or "What a wonderful meal," is a simple way of recognizing a person's gifts or passions, and affirming the person in her desire to host, help, and value her family. Recognizing the voices and talents that individuals bring to mutual interactions aids in making communities strong and progressive.

On the Margins of Space:
Paternalism and Youth Ministry

One of the challenges to encouraging discourse in any community is the tendency to paternalism and hierarchy.[3] This tendency can restrict the complexities of human discourse rather than allowing us to learn from them. The same tendency can equally instill in the members of a family or a larger community passivity, surrender, and the lack of responsibility. Critics of paternalism point to the cost that such a relationship carries, "namely, the negation of an active and responsible role for the child in her or his society."[4]

Paternalistic tendencies in youth ministry manifest themselves as the inability of adults to recognize youth as an active force in shaping human communities for the better. The paradigm of paternalistic youth ministry involves the systematic weakening of young people's agency and their social consciousness. This trend can be demonstrated by the passive, consumerist, avatar, and entertainment-hungry roles that youth are placed in as a result of "the detachment of young people from the material conditions — including economic, social, and political — of their communities."[5] The inability to articulate a role for youth in a community (be it a biological family, church family, or other contexts) stifles the growth of human communities because much of their energy goes to segregating youth from the larger societal habitat and the responsibilities attached to it, instead of integrating them.

Paternalistic tendencies in youth ministry are supported by developmental theories of the human life cycle, together with sociocultural constructs of adolescence. Theories of human development offer categories such as children and youth; early, middle, and late adolescence; preteens and teenagers, etc., to describe supposedly distinct stages of the human life cycle.[6] While these categories are helpful in describing and understanding the physical and mental qualities and behaviors that are not the same as those of adults, the same categories lead us to understand the adolescent population in contrast to adults. Adolescents *are* what the adults are *not*. In other words, the categories imply that young people are the lesser adults, since the adults are the norm for reasoning, conduct, and initiatives. Sharing commons, which is quintessentially about deliberately gathering together voices of different people, does not equate well with paternalism, which deliberately marginalizes or completely ignores their voices and leaves them adrift instead of according them a mooring, room at the table along with all the others.

Youth formation is often seen as the task of bringing youth to the level of adults. This presupposition can be ambiguous if society loses its common understanding of what the norms, behavior, or expectations of being adult look like. Having babies or holding a job does not convincingly constitute the grounds for being an adult. Having a degree from school (be it high school or college), driving a car, or wearing adult attire does not distinguish between adulthood and adolescence adequately, either. In contemporary U.S. society these cultural roles become quite blurred when, for example, a sixteen-year-old has a baby while her mom (the baby's grandmother) returns to college to earn a degree.

Fashion and cosmetics blur the boundaries further still. The latest plastic reconstructive surgeries prolong both men's and women's physical stage of young adulthood, helping them, perhaps, to own and savor youth once more. In her short reflection on what it means to be a grandmother, Wanda Mitchell shares the following:

> I brace myself against the counter while squinting my eyes at the face in the mirror. How could this woman possibly be a grandmother? She looks nothing at all like the grandmother who had been in my childhood. This woman doesn't have a speck of gray in her hair. And there is not a trace of wrinkles or age spots to be seen. Of course, to be fair, my grandmother didn't have fifty different boxes of hair coloring conveniently awaiting her at the grocery store or the wonderful selection of anti-aging creams that stand lining my counter like good little soldiers. Still it is difficult to believe that I have earned this title of "Grandma."[7]

Her feelings demonstrate the nature of tensions in death- and nature-defying societies. In these societies the process of growth and the natural rhythms that accompany it are treated as properties of human life — as something that belongs to human life but does not control it. Christian belief in death losing its dominion over life that is eternally redeemed through Jesus Christ has been culturally appropriated by secular humanist philosophy. This philosophy believes in science, progress, and an enlightened human mind, and it offers people a sense of agency and a glimpse of immortality.

Structurally, adolescence is the stage before young adulthood. Its place in the hierarchy of human growth succumbs to the influences and control of a higher stage. But what if adolescence were not treated hierarchically? I suggest that the parameters of adulthood are defined by the integrity and genuineness with which an individual relates to the complexity of creation. Adults who disrespect fellow human beings, who exploit the earth, colonize the weak, yearn for conflict, and have dubious morals ought not to claim adulthood just because they have turned forty. Being adult is not the privilege of age. The quality of adult behavior is measured by its responsibility to other human beings and their needs, the needs of the communities, diverse cultures, and earth with its fauna and flora. Being adult is the virtue of practice. If adulthood is not conceived merely in terms of developmental dynamics but equally in terms of manifested qualities and attitudes toward human society on the part of a person, then adults and youth are on a common journey to seek, shape, and share a common humanity. The practice of sharing commons pursues this goal by creating opportunities for mutual interactions between youth and adults. In the following pages I will discuss one of them: mentoring.

Mentoring

In the American movie *Gran Torino,* the actor Clint Eastwood plays a Korean war veteran named Walt Kowalski, a rugged, grumpy old man, who finds himself living next to an Asian family. Despite his biases and calling people racist names, he gradually warms up to the charm, spontaneity, and warmth of this family's teenage daughter and strikes up a friendship with her shy and withdrawn brother, Tao. Walt begins to mentor Tao, building up Tao's confidence regarding girls, his peers, and himself. The old man teaches Tao how to use common tools, to work manually, and to help his neighbors with minor repairs. In the process of mentoring, the main character learns things about himself: he is told by teenagers that he is a good man despite playing tough and racist; when moving a refrigerator, Tao shows Walt that he can no longer do the physically demanding things he used to do and that he needs to ask for Tao's help. As the two interact, they create rhythms and spaces for a mentoring relationship that gives this teenager the opportunity to ask for direction in his young life and Walt the opportunity to offer and act on his advice to Tao. Mentoring in this movie unfolds as a mutual enterprise between two culturally, ethnically, and generationally distant persons that begins with Walt discovering his capacity for care and concern for the young and with Tao seeking a male role model, structure, and friend. The movie suggests that mentoring is not a tool with which to forge a new person; rather, it is a journey of friendship and discovering the gifts that the persons have been endowed with and the ways to put the gifts into place to benefit the communities around them.

Involvement with youth is generally looked upon favorably by the broader U.S. society. The concept of mentoring youth through meaningful relationships is supported and welcomed by 75 percent of adults, though less than 35 percent actually practice it.[8] People's good intentions are hindered by various sociocultural forces: long working hours and a general climate of busyness (see chapter 1), the professionalization of child and youth formation, fear of youth, and the inaccessibility of youth. Suburban architecture does not always create easy venues for intergenerational mingling, either. U.S. suburbia nests families with children, while downtown condos welcome singles, and assisted living facilities are for the elderly. People's communities tend to be further segregated by ethnicity or even political views. Unstructured moments or spaces for striking up friendships with the young become infrequent. The institutions in U.S. society that continue to provide steady and structured spaces for youth and adults to come together are school, church, and the nonprofits (YMCA, Young Life, etc.). Yet as child care has become more professionalized and guarded (for example, through safe sanctuary movements in the churches), legal precautions are required to carry it out. These can act as reasons why some adults do not become involved. For example, the amount of paperwork required to enter a mentoring program with a school can deter or give pause to would-be volunteers. Mass media, too, are criticized for focusing on the sensational and negative aspects of the adult-youth involvement "such as the coverage given widespread sexual abuses by Catholic priests, or allegations of abuse by celebrities such as Michael Jackson."[9] Renting a garage apartment from a family with children can involve checking a prospective tenant's credit or even a criminal history record to ensure the safety of their children. Mentoring scenarios such as that depicted in *Gran Torino* do not necessarily affirm customary neighborhood practices; rather, the movie uses this mentoring relationship to challenge the audience to think about their own practices of sharing commons across generations, ethnicity, and economic status.

In addition to sociocultural pressures that surround mentoring initiatives, a person's misunderstanding of the nature of mentoring can also lead to mentoring failing, like a failed enterprise. The corporate model of mentoring focuses on "training for specific skills, preparation for working on a key project, or orientation to equip an individual to assume new job responsibilities."[10] Such a model therefore emphasizes values of efficiency, management, assignments, agenda, etc. These mentoring relationships tend to be hierarchical, with attempts to conform the other person to the mentor's ways of thinking and doing. Mentors who embrace solely a programmatic style of mentoring, which they use to instruct, impart information, or enhance tactics and strategies to meet particular goals and relational styles, fairly soon become discouraged. Their mentees feel commodified and not part of the process. Losing voice along with the status of partner and the sense of agency in the process makes it an alienating and self-deprecating experience.

When mentoring youth, many of the corporate models of mentoring are subconsciously or even consciously used. The age difference apparently gives adults the right to relate to young people on the basis of dominance, defining the sense of who they are and what they need to do — *for* them rather than *with* them. However, this is not the main challenge that mentoring youth has to reckon with. The greater challenge is the growing divisions between the differing kinds of knowledge, experience, and the cultural values the adults and young people hold. This division has been accelerated by new paradigms of living that emphasize global citizenship, technology, the online world, a redefinition of institutions such as marriage and family, leaps in science that as yet often lack interpretive ethical frameworks, and so forth. The parents or the grandparents' ability to pass on a piece of advice, values, or expertise is limited by this fast-moving world. A person's meaningful response to the scientific and moral expansion of human energy to far-fetched horizons surely requires a fresh lens to imagine, interpret, and live with the challenges and possibilities of the new era. The gap between the present and the futuristic reality that is being bridged by scientific progress carries an enormous irony. That is to say, the gap between what is and what can become diminishes with science and technology only to give rise to another gap: the gap between the human experience of progress and the ability of humans to adapt to it.

The challenge to mentoring is that the old have skills for which youth do not always have a need. (For example, teaching youth how to write letters is dismissed as an obsolete art because of widespread electronic communication.) Or the old do not always have the experience that youth want. (For example, advice about living or traveling to a foreign country might not be possible for mentors to give if they have limited experience of it.) The insecurity regarding the skills that the young need or want, or values that meaningfully address global world challenges, discourages people from mentoring. Youth are very clear in their abrupt, rebellious way about what they do or do not want or need.

These concerns raise the question about the nature of mentoring. Is the mentoring process about passing on to youth a set of specific skills, like in an apprenticeship? Is it about being present and modeling values and approaches to life? Or is it about building community? In this chapter I propose to treat mentoring as the process of creating a beat — a beat in life that brings regularity, feels natural, and generates new postures. This beat can provide youth with an implicit, almost subconscious life orientation, something they draw on or recall as a way of being, relating, and accruing knowledge in the world over the course of their life.

Beats in Jesus' Ministry:
Spiritual Practices: Reading John 13:1–17

What passage in the Bible can illustrate my concept of beat or natural rhythms in people's lives? To introduce this discussion, I turn to John 13:1–17. This passage from John's Gospel talks about Jesus washing his disciples' feet. It conveys themes of servanthood, humility, and postures. These themes are reenacted in worship on Maundy Thursday by the congregations of various denominations who practice Jesus' command to wash each other's feet. Maundy Thursday is the day in Holy Week that precedes Good Friday, the day of Jesus' crucifixion. Before Jesus washes his disciples' feet, they have the Last Supper together. The night before his own death, Jesus Christ leaves his disciples life-preserving and life-sustaining rhythms. Washing the feet, that is to say, becomes the means through which Christ not only teaches his disciples the value of servanthood but also through which he creates the rhythm of spiritual and liturgical life that preserves his teaching and actions.[11] I call this rhythm a *practice*. The spiritual practices in general are longstanding legacies of Christ's actions that are kept alive, are remembered and invoked through our communal participation in them. Such spiritual practices bind Christians into a distinctive body and a distinctive way of life.

My understanding of the concept of spiritual practices builds further upon the work of Christian educators like Craig Dykstra, David White, Kenda Dean, and others. Dykstra defines practices as "those cooperative human activities through which we, as individuals and as communities, grow and develop in moral character and substance."[12] Let me unpack this definition and highlight the key characteristics of a spiritual practice.

First, a spiritual practice is a communal way of doing things together.

Second, engaging in a spiritual practice pursues the goal of shaping and eliciting a moral response from the participants.

Third, when we participate in a spiritual practice, we actualize the intrinsic value of this practice.

Fourth, a spiritual practice is never only a once-in-a-life time activity. Practice becomes practice when we continue to repeat it.

Fifth, a spiritual practice needs to be tested and evaluated in the light of a contemporary situation of a community or an individual.

These characteristics can be further illuminated by suggesting a particular practice such as that of reading Scripture.

The first point suggests that a faith practice is communal. Whether we read Scripture as a family around the table or as a Bible study group in a church or in a dorm room, we take turns reading, we offer our insights, we raise our questions, we argue our points energetically, and we listen. Our communal reading renders it a practice because we cooperate and help each other to reflect on and understand what we read. However, there are other practices that we do on our own; we can read Scripture on our own, we can pray on our own. And yet these practices are also communal, in the sense that they are practiced in relationship with the Trinitarian God.

The second point suggests that a faith practice leads us toward a moral response. When we engage in the reading of Scripture, our capacities for doing good, for making right choices and for understanding why we ought to make a right choice are enlarged. Scripture provides insights into the human condition and reveals the ways in which God in Christ interacts with and transforms human beings. Witnessing to good and evil, tragedy and hope, sin and forgiveness, trust and doubt, the scriptural narratives offer us a motivational framework to strive for good, with God's Word being the primary agent of formation and transformation.

The third point suggests that by participating in a faith practice, we bring out its intrinsic value. What is valuable about the reading of Scripture? When we read Scripture, we are unleashing God's power into the world. We find a concrete illustration of this in Genesis 1:3: "Then God said, 'Let there be light; and there was light.'" When God proclaims God's Word, this Word becomes a live reality. And so do we. When we proclaim the Word, we make the Word alive. Or let's take another practice. What is the value of prayer? It is to trust and rely upon God. Or what is the value of forgiveness? It is to bring about reconciliation and peace. By praying or forgiving we invite the spiritual presence of God the Holy Spirit to make the realities of trust or reconciliation happen in our lives.

The fourth point suggests that a faith practice needs to be repeated. We probably all know the proverb: practice makes perfect. The continuous repetition of a faith practice — in the case of my illustration, the reading of Scripture — helps us grow in our faith. It helps us become better or more authentic in reenacting the values of the Christian faith. As Christians, we strive to become more compassionate, more forgiving, more loving disciples of Christ. But reading a scriptural passage once will not make us more compassionate. Our formational and transformational encounter with God in Christ occurs as we engage in a patient process of participation in the spiritual practices. When we become faithful practitioners of a faith practice, we engage in an activity that gives rhythm, meaning, and purpose to our lives.

The fifth point suggests that a faith practice needs to be tested. The ability of any practice to structure people's lives purposefully depends on its relevance for them. By testing a practice, I do not suggest that we disregard the history and tradition of the Christian church that serves as the primary well from which Christians draw their faith practices. Rather, testing a practice means to bring our reading of Scripture into a dialogue with present-day issues from our context. For example, how do adolescents read the passages about humility, giving up wealth, or discipleship when mainstream North American society celebrates the values of success, wealth, and pride? When we read Scripture through the lens of our race, gender, family tradition, or economic status, we make the Christian tradition so much more alive. Dykstra argues that this dialogue between Scripture, history, and tradition of the Christian church on the one hand and our living situation on the other helps to enlarge and even correct the Christian practices of faith.

The list of Christian spiritual practices is not a closed one. It is a wide open list to which we can add and modify as we converse with our contemporary situation. In summary, Christian spiritual practices initiate us into relationship with Christ and the church. They help us grow in the virtues of the Christian faith. (Our growth in these virtues is an engaging process that has us interact with self, neighbor, and the world in response to the living Word of God.) They help commit our hearts, minds, and bodies to God in Christ. They invest us with a purpose, a focus, and a virtuous life that is centered on the Word; and they invite the spiritual presence of the Trinitarian God into our lives.

Mentoring in the Spirit of Kitchen Table Ministry

Mentoring in the spirit of kitchen table ministry seeks to establish a trustworthy relationship between youth and adults. Its goal is not to create a malevolent friendship in which adult figures pursue a personal agenda and try to conform youth to their ways of thinking and doing. Nor is the goal of mentoring to create a benevolent friendship in which adult figures provide excesses of freedom to youth, leaving youth to their own devices. Rather, the goal of mentoring is to craft friendship in the mutual discovery of gifts, support, and learning from one another. Space plays an important role in this process.

When we mentor youth in the Word of God, we try to engage in practices that will prompt youth to change their physical and spiritual postures. The Word of God orchestrates our mental, emotional, spiritual, and physical movements. In doing so, it creates spaces for inviting others, whether neighbors or strangers, to come in. When we participate in the spiritual practices or sacraments, we submit ourselves to the playful work of the Holy Spirit who changes our physical and spiritual parameters. Families can use space to emphasize the rhythm of their daily lives, such as having a meal together. Families can also use space such as the kitchen to emphasize postures that convey attention to one another, such as sitting together around the table, instead of having something quick to eat while standing by the refrigerator. Families can use space to open themselves to otherness and difference through hospitality.

Using Space and Bodily Postures in John 13:1–17

Looking at the biblical text of John 13:1–17 from a Christian education perspective, I focus on bodylines and changing posture as "teaching methods" that Jesus employs to instruct and manifest to his disciples the values of servanthood and humility. Through washing their feet, Jesus reconfigures the bodies of his disciples.[13] And through reconfiguring their physical bodies, Jesus shapes his followers into a distinctive body. When his hands wash the feet of Peter, it confuses his friend, who was used to kissing and bowing at the feet of the one he saw as the Messiah. After Peter initially refuses to have his feet washed, Jesus tells him: "Unless I wash you, you have no share with me." Unless Peter allows himself (both mentally and physically) to place his feet into Jesus' hands, he is not able to share in his body. Sharing in the body of Jesus Christ implies putting on Jesus' embodied ways of treating fellow human beings. For Peter, sharing in the body of his Teacher requires Peter's surrender of cultural patterns of thinking and doing. Having his feet washed by Jesus requires that Peter submit to Jesus' will despite the cultural norms. We, too, humbly surrender to the will of our Lord when we allow our bodies to be reconfigured.

After washing his disciples' feet, Jesus returns to the table and asks his disciples: "Do you know what I have done to you?" "You call me Teacher and Lord — and you are right, for that is what I am. So, if I, your Lord and Teacher, have washed your feet, you also ought to wash one another's feet." In washing his disciples' feet, Jesus does more than just setting the example of servanthood. Jesus exchanges his bodylines with the disciples. In other words, Jesus marks the disciples as his own, as human beings who share in his own holy and eternal being. This wonderful "exchange," as Martin Luther calls it, during which Christ exchanges his purity and innocence for the stains of human sin, culminates on the cross. In this act of Christ's own bodily reconfiguration, he closes the space between God and sinful humanity. Our ability to create spaces for others is a result of Christ closing spaces between God and us first.

Using Space and Bodily Postures in the Movie *Gran Torino*

In *Gran Torino,* Walt Kowalski enters into a friendship with an Asian family in an absurd sort of way. He defends his personal space (his front yard) with a gun, and in doing so saves Tao from the gang members who try to kidnap him. Trying to close off his territory from the influences of neighbors and the outside world, Kowalski has, in an unsophisticated and paradoxical way, opened his space to other uses: friendship, thanks, visits, meals, and gifts from his Asian neighbors. This reversal of how his space functions — from excluding people to including them — is a thoughtful metaphor. It was not the space per se that changed the petulant old man; rather it was the result of an action by the Asian family who responded to Walt's use (or defense) of his personal space with hospitality and thanksgiving. Spaces can be transformative in combination with the practices and actions with which we fill them.

Using space and bodily postures as tools of formation

Physicality of the space and bodylines of human postures are important teaching tools through which we can convey values and forge new patterns of human relationships. When Jesus sat and had a meal with his disciples, he emphasized the equality of the divine image that is imprinted upon human beings by God in Christ regardless of their age, status, or physical and intellectual capacities. Adults and youth are equal in terms of their share in the divine image, and this truth is sealed by Christ through various examples, one of them being table fellowship with persons of unequal status. Mentoring processes that draw upon the paradigm of the kitchen table regard interaction between youth and adults as one in which both parties can sit *together* rather than *apart*.

Engaging youth with a faith perspective can begin with as simple a reflection as evaluating spaces in which a family is able to spend time together. In my first chapter, I discussed kitchen designs and their ability to draw family members together for mutual fellowship. Evaluating its kitchen in particular, a family is encouraged to pay attention not only to the working functionality of the kitchen space, but also to its social functionality. For example, islands in the kitchens assist in providing extra space for food preparation or in delineating a working area from a family area. Some islands take on the seating function around which a family can have a meal; others just serve as a quick and convenient station to prepare snacks, and lunch bags. The way eating stations are arranged across a family's dwelling also influence sitting postures and patterns of communication among individual family members. If families have only an island in the kitchen and a sofa in the family room, the tendency is to eat on the sofa in front of TV. This arrangement reduces the possibility for an attentive conversation. If families clutter their kitchen/dining table with laptops, mail, and school-related items, they can malform this eating space into a workstation even if they clear the table for the meal. Standing by the microwave or island and eating, or sitting on the sofa in front of the TV have become common modes of eating, especially if family members are in a hurry or eat alone.

What do these sitting and eating arrangements model to youth? What kind of implicit messages are coded in regular eating on the sofa or at a cluttered table? Can these postures be conducive to sharing God's Word? Families and communities who engage in the hospitable and transformative nature of God's Word do so by modeling the sacrament of the Eucharist. By having a family meal the adults nurture children in the memory, experience, and image of divine care and love. The metaphorical representations of the kitchen table reenact and embody the realities of the Eucharistic table such as divine hospitality, our remembering of God's redemptive action in Christ, God's remembering us in the act of uniting us around the table, divine playfulness. Divine playfulness refers to how God is able to transform Christ's body into spiritual fellowship or church. To understand the significance of the Eucharist, then, is to understand it as a creative action of the Trinitarian God to form spiritual fellowship that believers re-create every day as a church, a congregation, or a family. When families sit down at their kitchen tables, they can remember and reenact this act of divine playfulness.

When a family sits down at the table, it creates opportunities to bring Christ-like hospitality to the table: to bless the table and food, welcome family members, have the family members face one another, allow family members to serve one another, and ask questions about each other's lives. So encourage your family to distribute hospitality tasks among its members equally: Ask a different member of the family to pray, change serving modes (who brings food to the table, and how it is served), change sitting options (you can have a seat of honor for family members to whom you want to show particular love, respect, or encouragement), and be playful around the table (for example, by asking how many people Jesus sat with, who these people were, and what Jesus' message was, in order to stimulate curiosity about Bible).

Using Natural Rhythms

Mentoring in the spirit of the kitchen table suggests the use of spaces and natural rhythms of life. Natural rhythms of life can be used as vehicles for initiating conversations, building relationships, and creating moorings. Moorings ground a person's life with a sense of identity and are created through rhythmical actions of one's family, church, or neighborhood. For example, when a family moves too much, a geographical place loses its ability to ground individuals with a sense of belonging. Physical, mental, or spiritual moorings, I suggest, are developed through pulses of a family life. Jesus Christ and his followers did not live a settled life. As Jesus traveled with his disciples, the identity of the group was based on Jesus' proclamation of good news and the rhythms of his ministry (e.g., having meals, teaching, healing). The spiritual moorings of his followers were tied to a narrative that disciples were able to recount, and to the practices they and the early church were reenacting (e.g., meals, teaching, and preaching).

When I was explaining this concept to my students, one of them shared with the class that one of the natural rhythms her family had when she was a teenager was going to the mall on the weekend. Good and honest conversations between her and her parents occurred during the car ride and a stroll through the mall. Another of my students offered this example: His teenage son comes home with a group of his friends, and they like to gather in the kitchen while Mom fixes snacks for them. They hang out around the refrigerator; they joke and talk. These moments are usually times when he and his wife feel that the teenagers are most open, and the parents learn most about what is going on in their son and his friends' lives.

So the first step in mentoring youth is to create a trustworthy relationship by capitalizing on the rhythms of life as a family (e.g., going to a mall, bowling, a restaurant, a trip, eating dinner together, etc.). Each family can be encouraged to identify the rhythms in their life that feel natural, welcoming, and open. Even the more rigid forms of mentoring between adults and youth such as those at school or church need to look for a beat that feels natural to youth. One volunteer in the mentoring program in the church complained about his inability to connect with a young boy with whom he was paired. After a period of much frustration, the two of them were driving in the car together and began to talk about basketball, the boy's great passion. It was this conversation that generated an opening for a closer relationship, trust, and friendship.

Using Life Situations

When we mentor youth in the spirit of the kitchen table, we offer them a guiding narrative that can replace fragmented cultural narratives. This narrative is based on Scripture, and the adults offer youth a guiding narrative by engaging life situations with Scripture. Kitchen table ministry emphasizes the act of correlating life situations with Scripture. The question is how the families can take the step from discussing real-life situations that carry possible ethical implications to discussing matters of faith. Going back to the discussion between my niece and her grandmother, or between Jessie and her mother in the third chapter, I suggest that there are two possible follow-up scenarios. First, with any life situation that lends itself to ethical reflection, parents can emphasize Scripture as the source of ethical guidance and insight. Nonverbally — using the philosophy of the space — they can do it by the place where they position the Scripture. Central locations for certain pieces of the furniture such as the TV or computer bombard family members' senses and implicitly teach children and youth certain values. But where do families keep the Scripture? Is it in plain sight of the family so it can serve as a constant reminder of God's Word? Is it tucked away in an obscure place? If the Bible is kept where the family gathers (in the kitchen, on the coffee table in front of the sofa, or in the room or on the bookshelf of their child), Daniela's grandmother or Jessie's mother can reach for a Bible right after the meal and together look up what Scripture says on a particular subject. Second, they can have a follow-up discussion in the girls' rooms after dinner, reading the Bible together. The challenge of the first option is that the adults might be hesitant to look for a Biblical passage on the spot with their youth because they feel that they do not know what passage exactly to go to. During the week, they also might feel pressured for time, or they might lack focus and energy. This scenario also requires that youth are accustomed to sitting at the table even after the family is through with the meal. (More often than not teenage children leave the table as soon as they are done with the meal.) They also must be accustomed to Bible readings as part of the family meal. The second option provides time and opportunity to return to an issue with greater thoughtfulness and depth. However, it loses the immediacy of the moment and the window of opportunity to pursue the issue from a scriptural perspective. Waiting for a follow-up discussion requires more intentionality and determination on the part of a parent, and so one runs the risk of forgetting about it entirely.

If parents worry about their biblical preparedness, I argue that the solution is not so much about using the Bible as a self-help genre. Engaging a real-life issue with a faith perspective does not require that people find a particular verse that will remedy the situation; rather, the exercise is about reading a variety of passages and trying to understand the nature of God in Christ. Faith formation as I present it relies upon helping adolescents to create a faith-based framework that can guide them through various dilemmas, such as fitting in, being a good friend, or finding a good friend. Framing real-life issues with questions about God does not distract. It moves discussion about fashion or hazing to a larger cosmological ground. For the adolescent youth the subject matter of their stories involves the drama of their relationships, grades, sports, or expectations of adults. Without a guiding interpretative framework, the dramas of adolescent life can easily be experienced only at the level of intense feelings, hurt, or broken relationships instead of opportunities for reflection and charting a response in one's own words or actions.

Adults might worry about this not being a sufficient structure for their conversations and mentoring, but I suggest that using the liturgical rhythms of the church calendar (e.g., Advent, Lent, and the practices accompanying these periods, such as devotional and Bible readings) can provide an initial structure, intentionality, and practices for developing the habits of kitchen table ministry. The goal of kitchen table talk is to foster familiarity with biblical imagery, language, and stories. During the week when families feel overwhelmed by daily agendas, I suggest that they fill their dinner with "biblical snapshots" — a few words that lift up some aspect of divine actions (e.g., hospitality, faithfulness, sacrifice, deliverance). An example of a Biblical snapshot goes something like this:

The parent might say, "Here at the table we celebrate divine hospitality. It begins in the garden with Adam and Eve. God provided for them and God continues to provide for us." The parent can mention other instances of feeding God's people such as the Israelites in the desert or Jesus' feeding miracles. The parent can retell the biblical story in his or her own words. These brief accounts of God's story and the story of God's people help orient the family toward the images and language with which to frame the discussion of real-life situations. In other words, the transition from a secular framework of mind to a Christian one can be aided by these gentle reminders of God's presence in the lives of people both in the Bible and in the twenty-first century United States.

If Daniela's or Jessie's family were to introduce such God talk into their dinners, their discussions of fashion or hazing could more easily be molded by deeper questions such as these: In what image is God in Christ forming us? What does God in Christ call us to do? Does God in Christ call us to respond? These questions do not require that a parent, a grandparent, or a caretaker hastily search for a scriptural passage on clothes or hazing. Rather, the questions might spur curiosity in teenagers, provide the freedom and motivation to read the Bible later, and open the space for wrestling with their conscience. I admit that the responses to reading a Biblical passage may not speak directly to what kind of fashion to wear or what to say when somebody bullies you; rather, they provide youth with the framework of mind and heart to respond to these situations in their own words and actions. Having a biblical framework acts as a compass to help youth navigate the dilemmas of the adolescent world.

Taking Tables Outside...

At the beginning of this chapter, I explained that the practice of sharing commons initiates and models human fellowship to youth. In part this practice responds to a limited sample of people with which youth interact (e.g., peers, members of virtual communities, even the members of one's own family who can be ethnically homogenous). The goal of this practice cannot be fully completed without the assistance and involvement of the family with other human communities. The practice pushes kitchen table ministry out to broader contexts of human interactions such as church and its various ministries. One of the ways I envision this is having a roundtable ministry: on at least one night a week the family shares its dinnertime with youth and various other members of the congregation. Given the fact that even churches oftentimes represent a homogenous sample of the population, the roundtables might extend an invitation to the more diverse neighborhood population and other churches. Churches' Wednesday suppers can once a month be turned into an evening of "fellowship with the stranger." Like Jesus Christ who traveled with his disciples through various villages and towns, a youth group can visit and share a meal with folks from other congregations or invite folks to their congregation.

During the roundtable ministry, regular meals serve the function of discovering what connects and unites people. Coming from a different culture myself, I learned to recognize that when people point to universal features of humanity (such as what makes people happy or sad, hobbies, eating practices, travels), people feel that they share more in common than they previously thought they did. In churches connected through a biblical narrative, the roundtable ministry can encourage a mutual recognition of the unifying story. Surely different denominations have different interpretations of any particular story, but I am not calling for people to engage in zealous theological disputes. The goal of sharing commons is to share life and Bible together as human family. This practice provides the grounds from which youth can embark on the journey of discovering the variety and richness of humanity.

You can continue kitchen table ministry by:

◆ *Evaluating your opportunities to meet youth*

1. As a family, think about the occasions you have to meet teenage children other than your own. Are these occasions limited to brief encounters, such as when a teenager brings home her or his friends? Or are they regular and consistent

meetings with youth during which relationships can be formed and cultivated?

2. Along with your teenage children map the demographics of your street or block and ask yourselves: How many families do we know in our neighborhood? How many of them have teenage children? I am quite certain that you know other parents from your children's schools, teacher-parent conferences, or sports. Your daughter or son may likewise have lots of friends through their online networking. But how many of them do you know and meet in the physical proximity of your house?

◆ Establish a Round Table Ministry Person

1. Organize kitchen table youth ministry through your congregation. Offer to host a meal with youth from your congregation once a month in your home. Focus on having a meal around the table. Try to invite youth who are not biologically related to you. Arrange with other parents in the congregation to host similar meals and invite different youth. Invite congregational members of different generations to join you. Make the company around your table as intergenerational as you can.

2. Organize round table ministry in your congregation: meet around round tables and food. Focus on the less privileged families and families whose children might not experience family meals because of their family's busy schedule or lack of resources. Remind the participants that the round tables model Eucharistic fellowship.

◆ Use Space

1. Use space in your home. Notice whether your home space is inviting to God's Word. Choose what the central locations of your home are and begin placing religious artifacts in those places. For example, place a Bible on the coffee

table in front of your TV. Try to visualize faith through positioning its symbols throughout the house where your family gathers. Pay attention to this symbolism and its effect on the family members. Has anybody noticed anything? If your house already has religious artifacts, can you teach faith tradition by using some of them? By having paintings, icons, or crosses in the bedrooms, the dining room, or the living room, can we call attention to them and generate discussion? Sometimes it is enough to be surrounded by religious symbolism, but if that symbolism becomes so familiar we no longer notice it, an intentional discussion about what the symbols mean can awaken us to it again.

2. Take your family to visit a cathedral or drive through the countryside to observe the churches. Notice what denominations the churches belong to. Kindle an interest in the Christian faith by paying attention to its architecture. Throughout the Middle Ages, church architecture with its stained-glass windows, sculptures, and symbolism were the chief means by which to educate people, especially illiterate people, in the Christian faith. What can you learn about the church by paying attention to the physical space and ornamentation of your local churches?

Chapter Six

To What End?

WHEN DEALING WITH the questions of Christian formation, one question comes to the fore: To what end are we forming our children and youth? The Didache, the second-century text of the Christian church on teaching, talks about two ways: the way of life and the way of death. Christian education and formation needs to be the way of life. It needs to shape the church into the instrument of God's sustaining grace in faith, of God's reconciliation with humanity in Christ's death on the cross, and of God's sanctification of creation in the transformative work of the Holy Spirit. And it needs to shape individuals into grateful recipients of a divine grace that calls for a personal response.

Christian education as a way of life is deeply embedded in the living Word of God both as the written word and as the incarnated reality in Jesus Christ. The way of life comes with the Word befriending us, transforming us, and helping to orient us in our relationship with God, with our neighbor, and with the world in general. When Martin Luther developed the educational resources for the laity and the clergy such as the Small and Large Catechisms, he made God's Word the primary teacher. Luther argued that the Word as the written word not only convicted people of their sinfulness, but it also prepared them to be receptive of God's grace, to rely on God's promises, and to grow in trust in God in Christ. Engagement with the Word of Scripture was like a journey throughout which one grew in the life of faith from the point of the realization of one's sinfulness to the point of entrusting oneself to the fullness of God's grace in Christ.

Such growth in the life of faith is marked by a person's ability to have a deeper, more authentic, but also more responsive relationship with God and with the larger world. It is marked by one's ability to produce the fruits of faith or good works. Luther saw good works as necessary for the life of faith if these are directed toward the outside world, saying, "For faith without works is dead and worth nothing."[1] For Luther and his followers good works can never be interpreted other than as the fruits of faith. Good works do not justify; rather they follow a justified heart.

Luther spoke of the fruits of faith in terms of vocation. The nature of vocation lies in a person's transformed heart that generates his/her response in faith and love to this marvelous act of divine transformation. In vocation we respond to God's gift of grace in Jesus Christ and testify to the living presence of the Word within us. The role of vocation is to tie our response to God's transforming grace in Christ with the way we demonstrate this response. Vocation has no limits. We have a vocation by being a good student, a caring daughter, a devoted teacher, or a skilled surgeon. Through what we are or what we do we manifest an attitude of what it means to live under divine grace.

Vocation is the end to which we ought to form our children and youth. When we pursue vocation as the goal of spiritual formation, we help youth to live their lives in response to God's Word. We help them to write "a thank you note" to God in Christ; only they do not need a paper and pen, but rather they need their lives, attitudes, hearts, thoughts, words, and gifts to demonstrate this thankfulness. If we continue to entrust young people's lives to the Word of God, the transformative work of the Holy Spirit will make their vocation a creative, dynamic, and unique enterprise, underwritten by the gifts of the Holy Spirit and personal responsiveness. This further means that having a vocation is not limited to the concept of ordained ministry. Are you or your teenager gifted in particular ways? If you think about your gifts in terms of vocation, you think about the ways to put these gifts to good use to benefit the community around you. In the capacity of our vocation, we engage God's creation actively and imaginatively, using our human agency, that is, our reason, our will, our emotions. By adding layers of human faculties to a justified heart, a person grows in the life of faith.

In vocation then, we participate in the life of the Spirit. Christian educator Craig Dykstra suggests that formation in Christian faith occurs through this process of participation in the life of the Spirit.[2] Dykstra further asserts that we participate in the life of the Spirit through the community of faith.[3] Worship, sacraments, the acts of proclamation of the Word, and the practices of faith unleash the reality of God's love into the world by acting as "places where the power of God is experienced."[4] The places of encounter — for example, a church community with its actions, its hymns, its rituals, its acts of proclamation, and its practices — empower us to reenact, embody, and witness to God's radical order for creation.

In this book I have focused mainly on the experience of divine power through the embodied context, particularly as family fellowship around the kitchen table. The embodied context itself is not transformative unless it is filled with faith-based transformative practices. The practices of kitchen-table-based spiritual formation, I argue, help create encounters with the divine praxis of transformation and nurture by incarnating it through the human agents. I am aware of the risks that such a human act of incarnation carries within itself. That is to say, containing God's power and the sovereignty of divine praxis in embodied contexts such as kitchen table fellowship can easily become the expression of human praxis. And if we happen to model this divine praxis of nurture in insufficient or distorted ways (and as human beings who are ontologically sinful we will), we will inevitably teach and incarnate God's activity in a flawed way. Embodied grace is grace that comes to us through a multitude of channels — through the sacraments, through doctrine, through ecclesial community, *and* through table fellowship.

The value of Christian education and formation centered on the paradigm of the kitchen table is that it places children and youth under the grace of God through a family-style proclamation of the Word. This goal further means that children and youth learn to interact with the Word, engage the Word with their lives, and experience the transformative power of the Word. And they do it as a family. The Word becomes their teacher. Christian educators are there in order to mediate the nearness of the Word and to facilitate the teaching moments. Christian education and formation is then a family enterprise, grounded in the Word and dispensed with the grace of God through gracious relationships.

Christian education and formation needs to be a family enterprise (but not necessarily that of a biological family) to counteract the biological family's weakening capacity to provide a wholesome nurture for its children. Kitchen table youth ministry responds to various forms of youth abandonment by adults that can range from the lack of time to have regular conversations over family meals to the inability to provide for one's family and secure a safe environment for the growth of a child. The concept of abandonment does not imply a malevolent, intentional will on the part of the caretaker; rather, it is a by-product of societal pressures and lifestyle, for example, an intense work schedule or dependence on technology. As a result of fast-paced living, families often suffer from the lack of opportunities to articulate a vocational narrative based in God's Word of Scripture and are unable to implement practices to transmit it.

Kitchen table youth ministry calls for a network of support or a community of caring individuals because discerning a proper response to God's gift of grace goes far beyond individual capabilities. A youth might ask a question: What is divine grace? How do I know I have it? The means of channeling divine grace are important teaching tools that precede the articulation of a response. Of course, I am not advocating an evolutionary stimulus-response model. I am suggesting we involve youth in the practices of faith that dispense and mediate divine grace in more tangible ways.

The practices of faith can convey grace in intimate ways (prayer, contemplation) and communal ways (worship). Human response grows in the context of regular participation, the experience and proclamation of divine grace, orchestrated by the work of the Holy Spirit. An authentic vocational response cannot be induced, imposed, or curricularized, but, I believe, it can be nurtured, invoked, discussed, shown, and ultimately practiced with youth. Vocational response always calls for communities to encircle each other, and mainly youth, to generate the experience of divine grace and offer ways to interpret it and respond to it. This activity calls for space, relationality, and interaction among the members of a group (be it a family, a faith community, or some other small group). Kitchen table fellowship tries to combine these prerequisites into a way of discerning divine grace, reflecting on it, and articulating a response to it (which can be as simple as completing a school application with your teenagers and as complex as building moral character or spiritual life with your child). Vocation represents a spectrum of human responses grounded in the life-giving Word of God, and as our children grow in the life of faith, they — we hope — will grow in the complexity and intricacy of their manifestations of vocation. Ultimately, vocation is the work of God in Christ. We can participate in it by being faithful witnesses to the divine praxis of transformation. We bring this witness home to our kitchen tables by inviting God to dinner.

Notes

Chapter 1: Spiritual Formation at the Center of the Kitchen

1. The onset of abstract thought occurs between the late end of early adolescence (ten to twelve) and the beginning of middle adolescence (thirteen to fifteen).

2. James W. Fowler, *Stages of Faith: The Psychology of Human Development and the Quest for Meaning* (San Francisco: HarperSanFrancisco, 1995), 153.

3. Kenda C. Dean, *Practicing Passion: Youth and the Quest for a Passionate Church* (Grand Rapids, Mich.: Eerdmans, 2004), 180.

4. As representative works on the phenomenon of abandonment or separation, see Chap Clark, *Hurt: Inside the World of Today's Teenagers* (Grand Rapids, Mich.: Baker Academic), 2004; David Elkind, *The Hurried Child: Growing Up Too Fast Too Soon*, 3rd ed. (Cambridge, Mass.: Da Capo Press, 2007); Kenda Dean, *Practicing Passion: Youth and the Quest for a Passionate Church* (Grand Rapids, Mich.: Eerdmans), 2004.

5. Patricia Hersch, *A Tribe Apart* (New York: Ballantine Books), 1998.

6. Barry Taylor, *Entertainment Theology: New Edge Spirituality in a Digital Democracy* (Grand Rapids, Mich.: Baker Academic, 2008), 135–42.

7. Taylor discusses the movie *Waterworld* to illustrate a shift in people's skills and thinking through which they adjust to a completely liquified world. Ibid., 89–95.

8. Don S. Browning, *Equality and the Family: A Fundamental, Practical Theology of Children, Mothers, and Fathers in Modern Societies* (Grand Rapids, Mich.: Eerdmans, 2007), 56.

9. Quentin J. Schultze, *Habits of the High-Tech Heart: Living Virtuously in the Information Age* (Grand Rapids, Mich.: Baker Academic, 2002), 27.

10. Ibid., 40.

11. *www.pewinternet.org/pdfs/PIP_Networked_Family.pdf,* pp. 1–2; accessed on November 12, 2008.

12. Robert D. Putnam, *Bowling Alone: The Collapse and Revival of American Community* (New York: Simon & Schuster, 2000), 193.

13. Katherine Turpin, *Branded: Adolescents Converting from Consumer Faith* (Cleveland: Pilgrim Press, 2006), 32.

14. Browning, *Equality and the Family,* 53.

15. A teleological principle of natural selection can be illustrated by the case of sterile female ants. Charles Darwin first observed the paradox within the communities of social insects (such as ants) whose welfare depends upon effective labor division. The most effective workers appear to be sterile females. The stumbling block for Darwin and his theory was the question of the process that secures the continuity of sterile females, given the fact that sterility is that which disables females from laying eggs. Darwin discusses the wonder of natural selection since, in the strict genetic sense, this runs counter to the natural selection principle. Somehow natural selection continues to preserve genes that do not support further variations of certain species for the sake of mummifying or preserving a trait that is highly beneficial for the whole group. The criterion for preserving and multiplying the trait among the members of the group, even at the expense of suppressing or eliminating other traits, seems to be the wellbeing of the group. See Charles Darwin, *The Origin of Species* (New York: Gramercy Books, 1979), 262.

16. Nebraska's safe haven law has become a controversial piece of legislation. Since it does not state an age limit for a child, children up to age nineteen can be dropped off at medical centers. A well-known case is that of a father who gave up his nine children aged one to seventeen, unable to care for them after his wife died.

17. Elkind, *The Hurried Child,* xvi.

18. Clark, *Hurt,* 46.

19. Elizabeth F. Caldwell, *Making a Home for Faith: Nurturing the Spiritual Life of Your Children* (Cleveland: Pilgrim Press, 2000), vi.

20. Sharon Daloz Parks, "Household Economics," in *Practicing Our Faith: A Way of Life for a Searching People,* ed. Dorothy C. Bass (San Francisco: Jossey-Bass, 1997), 47.

21. bell hooks, *Yearning: Race, Gender, and Cultural Politics* (Boston: South End Press, 1990), 42.

22. Sharon Daloz Parks, "Home and Pilgrimage: Companion Metaphors for Personal and Social Transformation," *Soundings* 72, nos. 2–3 (Summer–Fall 1989): 304; quoted in Caldwell, *Making a Home for Faith*, 9.

23. Maggie Jackson, *What's Happening to Home? Balancing Work, Life, and Refuge in the Information Age* (Notre Dame, Ind.: Sorin Books), 2002.

24. Anecdotally, I know of women who mourn the loss of a family washing the dishes together that occurred with the arrival of dishwasher into kitchens. These women consider times when the children and their parents were cleaning up and washing dishes together as a special and quality time for family conversations. Having said this, neither Jackson nor I are calling for a return of the lifestyle that would enslave women among their aprons and pots and bury their aspirations, talents, intellect, and beauty as it has happened and continues to happen to women suffering under the patriarchal shackles of various societies.

25. Elkind, *The Hurried Child*, 20.

26. In the time period between 1965 and 2005, the number of hours spent on household duties by women fell from an average of 4.6 to 2.7 hours per day. Men's participation in household duties increased from 0.6 to 1.7 hours. See *www.pewinternet.org/pdfs/PIP_Networked_Family.pdf*, accessed on November 12, 2008.

27. Jackson, *What's Happening to Home?* 71.

28. Terence Conran, *Kitchens: The Hub of the Home* (New York: Clarkson Potter Publisher, 2002), 11.

29. Susan Maney Lovett, *The Smart Approach to Kitchen Design*, 3rd ed. (Upper Saddle River, N.J.: Creative Homeowner, 2006), 31.

30. *www.nkba.org/consumer_tools_statistics.aspx;* accessed on October 23, 2008.

31. *The Best of Signature Kitchens* (Upper Saddle River, N.J.: Creative Homeowner, 2005), 8.

32. *www.nkba.org/consumer_inspiration_2008_dc_winners.aspx;* accessed on October 27, 2008.

33. Statistics seem to document that behind the remodeling of the kitchen space lies the need for accommodating a family. Forty-three percent of families who remodel kitchens are families with teenage children or young adults, and 36 percent are "empty nester" families who want to have enough space for their children and grandchildren. See *www.nkba.org/consumer_tools_statistics.aspx;* accessed on October 23, 2008.

34. Lovett, *The Smart Approach to Kitchen Design*, 32.

35. The ideal triangle would require that the "distance between any pair of the three centers is no longer than 9 feet and no less than 4 feet." See Lovett, *The Smart Approach to Kitchen Design,* 40.

36. Christopher Alexander, *A Pattern Language: Towns, Buildings, Construction* (New York: Oxford University Press, 1977), 662.

37. Conran, *Kitchens*, 14.

38. Letty M. Russell, *Church in the Round: Feminist Interpretation of the Church* (Louisville: Westminster John Knox Press, 1993), 78.

39. Alexander, *A Patterned Language*, 698.

40. Conran, *Kitchens*, 11.

41. *www.casacolumbia.org/absolutenm/articlefiles/380–Importance %20of%20Family%20Dinners%20IV.pdf;* accessed March 11, 2008.

42. Miriam Weinstein, *The Surprising Power of Family Meals: How Eating Together Makes Us Smarter, Stronger, Healthier, and Happier* (Hanover, N.H.: Steerforth Press), 2005.

43. Miriam Weinstein writes that dining etiquette that, for example, teaches people to turn the knives toward the plate or not to raise forks while conversing and gesticulating aims at preventing people from harming one another. Similarly, having people sit down and face one another while having a meal as opposed to standing while eating, watching TV, or eating in one's own room teaches people the skills of bonding, listening, attentiveness, etc. See Weinstein, *The Surprising Power of Family Meals,* 89, 100.

44. Ibid., 116.

45. Michael Pollan, *In Defense of Food: An Eater's Manifesto* (New York: Penguin Press, 2008), 192.

46. Ibid., 183–205.

47. Putnam, *Bowling Alone*, 102.

48. Pollan, *In Defense of Food*, 189–90.

49. Weinstein, *The Surprising Power of Family Meals*, 139.

50. According to the Pew Internet and American Life Project, a family that tends to have family meals with its members every day or almost every day is in a parenting relationship with its child or children; females do it more often than males; family members who are not employed and seniors (sixty-five-plus) host family meals with most regularity. This research leaves in question the dinner patterns of working families. See *www.pewinternet.org/pdfs/PIP_Network_Family.pdf*; accessed on November 12, 2008.

51. James E. Loder, *The Logic of the Spirit: Human Development in Theological Perspective* (San Francisco: Jossey-Bass, 1998), 223.

52. Chap Clark and Dee Clark, *Disconnected: Parenting Teens in a MySpace World* (Grand Rapids, Mich.: Baker Books, 2007), 39.

53. Clark, *Hurt*, 109.

54. Paul Ricoeur, *History and Truth*, trans. Charles A. Kelbley (Evanston, Ill.: Northwestern University Press, 1965), 99.

55. Fred P. Edie, *Book, Bath, Table, and Time: Christian Worship as Source and Resource for Youth Ministry* (Cleveland: Pilgrim Press, 2007), 9.

Chapter 2: Table Fellowship: Real or Virtual?

1. Michael Bugeja, *Interpersonal Divide: The Search for Community in a Technological Age* (New York: Oxford University Press, 2005), 5.

2. James E. Loder, *The Logic of the Spirit: Human Development in Theological Perspective* (San Francisco: Jossey-Bass, 1998), 219, 223.

3. Evelyn Parker, "Theological Framework for Youth Ministry: Hope," in *Starting Right: Thinking Theologically about Youth Ministry*, ed. Kenda C. Dean, Chap Clark, and David Rahn (Grand Rapids, Mich.: Zondervan Publishing House, 2001), 265–76.

4. Loder, *The Logic of the Spirit*, 214.

5. Kenda C. Dean, *Practicing Passion: Youth and the Quest for Passionate Church* (Grand Rapids, Mich.: Eerdmans, 2004), 93–115.

6. Parker, "Theological Framework for Youth Ministry: Hope" in *Starting Right*, 265–76.

7. Richard R. Osmer, *Confirmation: Presbyterian Practices in Ecumenical Perspective* (Louisville: Geneva Press, 1996), 9–19.

8. James W. Fowler, *Stages of Faith: The Psychology of Human Development and the Quest for Meaning* (San Francisco: HarperSanFrancisco, 1981), 77.

9. Robert D. Putnam, *Bowling Alone: The Collapse and Revival of American Community* (New York: Simon & Schuster, 2000), 173.

10. Don Tapscott, *Growing Up Digital: The Rise of the Net Generation* (New York: McGraw-Hill, 1998), 237.

11. *www.pewinternet.org/pdfs/PIP_Networked_Family.pdf;* accessed on November 12, 2008.

12. Peggy Kendall, *Connected: Christian Parenting in an Age of IM and MySpace* (Valley Forge, Pa.: Judson Press, 2007), 48.

13. Tapscott, *Growing Up Digital,* 90–95.

14. Kendall, *Connected,* 51.

15. *www.cnn.com/2008/CRIME/11/21/webcam.suicide/index.html;* accessed on November 22, 2008.

16. *www.pewinternet.org/pdfs/PIP%20Cyberbullying%20Memo;* pdf, p. 4; accessed on November 12, 2008.

17. Ibid., 5, and Peggy Kendall, *Rewired: Youth Ministry in an Age of IM and MySpace* (Valley Forge, Pa.: Judson Press, 2007), 52.

18. When I created an avatar in the Second Life (a virtual community) in order to tour the Princeton University campus, I noticed how lonely my tour was. Strolling through the virtual campus, I did not meet anyone. When I teleported my avatar to another virtual community and attempted to enter a coffee shop, I was denied access because I was not a member of the group that typically met in and claimed that space. Physical proximity offers freedom to be part of human community because one is free in a real space and not sequestered by particular log-ins.

19. Robert D. Putnam and Lewis M. Feldstein, *Better Together: Restoring American Community* (New York: Simon & Schuster, 2003), 227.

20. Kendall, *Connected,* 63.

21. Ibid.

22. See chapter 1 for my discussion of this concept.

23. Bugeja, *Interpersonal Divide,* 103.

24. Quentin J. Schultze, *Habits of the High-Tech Heart: Living Virtuously in the Information Age* (Grand Rapids, Mich.: Baker Academic, 2002), 171.

25. Kendall, *Rewired,* 33.

26. The *New York Times* published a story about Thanksgiving dinner fellowship, titled "In Lean Times, Comfort in a Bountiful Meal."

The story featured one family among others that was struggling to put food on the table because of the father's sudden job loss. Sad news for this family was exacerbated by the way the father learned about it. On a Saturday he received an automated phone call announcing that he had been laid off from his job. The lack of courage on the part of the company to talk to its employee directly is ultimately the result of desubjectifying people, which occurs in the high-tech society driven mostly by mediated communication. See my discussion in the first chapter. For the story, go to *www.nytimes.com/2008/11/28/us/28thanks.html?emc=eta1;* accessed on November 28, 2008.

27. Kendall, *Rewired*, 64.

28. Schultze, *Habits of the High-Tech Heart*, 116.

29. Chap Clark, *Hurt: Inside the World of Today's Teenagers* (Grand Rapids, Mich.: Baker Academic, 2004), 145–57.

30. Chap Clark and Dee Clark, *Disconnected: Parenting Teens in a MySpace World* (Grand Rapids, Mich.: BakerBooks, 2007), 137.

31. Bugeja, *Interpersonal Divide*, 108.

32. Sociologist Robert Putnam calls these trends "cyberbalkanization," which causes virtual communities to become less diverse and pluralistic. This further means that people search and commune with others who are like them as opposed to others who are different. Virtual cultural immersion is then more about nurturing comfort with oneself than growth of oneself amid difference. See Putnam, *Bowling Alone*, 178.

33. Schultze, *Habits of the High-Tech Heart*, 59.

34. Michael Pollan, *In Defense of Food: An Eater's Manifesto* (New York: Penguin Press, 2008), 190.

35. *www.pewinternet.org/pdfs/PIP_Networked_Family.pdf,* p. 16; accessed on November 12, 2008.

36. The data from Putnam's research state that "81 percent of all Americans report that most evenings they watch TV, as compared with only 56 percent who talk with family members...[or] 27 percent who do household chores" (Putnam, *Bowling Alone*, 227).

37. Ibid., 223.

38. *www.pewinternet.org/pdfs/PIP_Networked_Family.pdf,* pp. 11–30; accessed on November 12, 2008.

39. Putnam, *Bowling Alone*, 100.

40. *www.pewinternet.org/pdfs/PIP_Networked_Family.pdf,* pp. 11–30; accessed on November 12, 2008.

41. Andrew Pettegree, *Reformation and the Culture of Persuasion* (New York: Cambridge University Press, 2005), 166.

42. Schultze, *Habits of the High-Tech Heart,* 64.

43. Bill Plotkin, *Nature and the Human Soul: Cultivating Wholeness and Community in a Fragmented World* (Novato, Calif.: New World Library, 2008), 138.

44. Richard E. Sclove, "Making Technology Democratic," in *Resisting the Virtual Life: The Culture and Politics of Information,* ed. James Brook and Ian A. Boal (San Francisco: City Lights, 1995), 85–105.

45. New patterns of social life, as influenced by technology, are not necessarily the problem, especially if they contribute to democratic features of society such as shared infrastructure or computerized civic engagement. However, if technology is misconstrued in its purpose (e.g., the partnership between a telecommunication industry and a government surveillance program of its citizens), it will enhance the economic and political might of selected sectors in society (e.g., the defense or marketing industries) at the expense of enhancing democracy. Technology driven by economic gains solely will diminish the strength of human villages by replacing them with the communities of special interests.

46. Schultze, *Habits of the High-Tech Heart,* 15–24.

47. *www.pewinternet.org/pdfs/PIP_Networked_Family.pdf,* p. 28; accessed on November 12, 2008.

48. Fred P. Edie, *Book, Bath, Table, and Time: Christian Worship as Source and Resource for Youth Ministry* (Cleveland: Pilgrim Press, 2007), 86.

49. Plotkin, *Nature and the Human Soul,* 182.

50. Aquinas, *God's Greatest Gifts: Commentaries on the Command-ments and the Sacraments,* trans. Joseph B. Collins (Manchester, N.H.: Sophia Institute Press, 1992), 84.

51. Aquinas, *Summa Theologiae: A Concise Translation,* ed. Timothy McDermott (Allen, Tex.: Christian Classics, 1989), 561.

52. Cristina L. H. Traina, "A Person in the Making," in *The Child in Christian Thought,* ed. Marcia J. Bunge (Grand Rapids, Mich.: Eerdmans, 2001), 111.

53. Ibid.

54. Edie, *Book, Bath, Table, and Time*, 39.

Chapter 3: The Practice of Table Talk: Tell Me a Story

1. Gerald Strauss, *Luther's House of Learning: Indoctrination of the Young in the German Reformation* (Baltimore: Johns Hopkins University Press, 1978), 125.

2. The effectiveness of family catechesis is evidenced in research conducted by Luther Seminary and Southwestern Seminary. The study concludes that a deep commitment of youth to faith is nurtured by a number of practices. According to this study, the practices most likely to help produce a deep faith are accrued in a family setting and through a family lifestyle that is centered around practicing a religious life actively. See Luther Seminary and Southwestern Seminary, "Factors in Youth and Young Adult Faith. Experience and Development: A Longitudinal Study," posted at *www.faithfactors.com/docs/Longdt.doc;* accessed on October 23, 2006.

3. Don S. Browning, *Equality and Family: A Fundamental, Practical Theology of Children, Mothers, and Fathers in Modern Societies* (Grand Rapids, Mich.: Eerdmans, 2007), 226.

4. William J. Bausch, *Storytelling: Imagination and Faith* (Mystic, Conn.: Twenty-Third Publications, 1984), 93.

5. Preserved Smith, *Luther's Table Talk* (New York: AMS Press, 1907), 103.

6. Cynthia Gordon, "Al Gore's Our Guy: Linguistically Constructing a Family Political Identity," in *Family Talk: Discourse and Identity in Four American Families*, ed. D. Tannen, S. Kendall, and C. Gordon (New York: Oxford University Press, 2007), 241.

7. See *www.storycorps.net* for an overview of history, mission, and goals of the project. See also Dave Isay, *Listening Is an Act of Love: A Celebration of American Life from the StoryCorps Project* (New York: Penguin Press, 2007). Isay is the founder of the StoryCorps project, and his book is the collection of the recorded stories throughout the United States.

8. Isay, *Listening Is an Act of Love*, 269.

9. Maureen O'Brien, "How We Are Together: Educating for Group Self-Understanding in the Congregation," in *Religious Education* 92, no. 3 (1997): 315–22.

10. Dori Baker and Joyce Mercer, *Lives to Offer: Accompanying Youth on Their Vocational Quest* (Cleveland: Pilgrim Press, 2007), 71–88.

11. Sarah Arthur, *The God-Hungry Imagination. The Art of Storytelling for Postmodern Youth Ministry* (Nashville: UpperRoom Books, 2007), 76.

12. Isay, *Listening Is an Act of Love*, 267.

13. Gordon D. Kaufman, *The Theological Imagination: Constructing the Concept of God* (Philadelphia: Westminster Press, 1981), 263–79.

14. Ibid., 274.

15. Bausch, *Storytelling*, 15–28.

16. Ibid., 19.

17. Mary Elizabeth Mullino Moore, *Teaching from the Heart: Theology and Educational Method* (Harrisburg, Pa.: Trinity Press International, 1998), 153.

18. Carol Lakey Hess, *Caretakers of Our Common House: Women's Development in Communities of Faith* (Nashville: Abingdon Press, 1997), 182–213.

19. Hess, *Caretakers of Our Common House*, 182.

20. Shoshana Blum-Kulka, *Dinner Talk: Cultural Patterns of Sociability and Socialization in Family Discourse* (Mahwah, N.J.: Lawrence Erlbaum Associates, 1997), 12, 15.

21. Smith, *Luther's Table Talk*, 11.

22. Kulka, *Dinner Talk*, 45.

23. Ibid., 52.

24. Ibid., 131.

25. Michael Riera, *Staying Connected to Your Teenager: How to Keep Them Talking to You and How to Hear What They're Really Saying* (Cambridge, Mass.: Perseus Publishing, 2003), 78.

26. Isay, *Listening Is an Act of Love*, 253.

27. Deborah Tannen, *You're Wearing That? Understanding Mothers and Daughters in Conversation* (New York: Random House, 2006), 62–63.

28. Psychologist Michael Riera suggests that in addition to the process of individuation that an adolescent daughter goes through, the mother-daughter relationship is influenced by hormonal changes of their bodies. Daughters learn to cope with their menstruation cycles, while mothers go through their menopause. These changes, too, are

responsible for generating a variety of anxious interactions between the two females. See Riera, *Staying Connected to Your Teenager*, 126.

29. Tannen, *You're Wearing That?* 17.

30. Ibid., 83.

31. For a discussion of the challenges to a father-daughter relationship, see Riera, *Staying Connected to Your Teenager*, 132–34.

32. Riera, *Staying Connected to Your Teenager*, 129.

33. As anecdotal evidence, I have overheard many arguments between adolescents and their parents at the center of which was the claim "I am not a child anymore."

34. Chap Clark and Dee Clark, *Disconnected: Parenting Teens in a MySpace World* (Grand Rapids: Baker Books, 2007), 142–43.

35. Ibid., 118.

36. Miriam Weinstein, *The Surprising Power of Family Meals: How Eating Together Makes Us Smarter, Stronger, Healthier, and Happier* (Hanover, N.H.: Steerforth Press, 2005), 122.

37. With abstract thinking, which emerges at the end of the early adolescence period, youth accrue the ability to think about their own thoughts, concepts, and abstract theories. This new mental competency enables them to engage in reflective thought the subjects of which can be relationships and abstract realities such as love, peace, justice, etc.

38. Riera, *Staying Connected to Your Teenager*, 173.

39. Carol Lakey Hess, "Ministry with Children and Youth," in *The Family Handbook*, ed. H. Anderson, D. Browning, I. Evison, M. Van Leeuwen (Louisville: Westminster John Knox Press, 1998), 133.

Chapter 4: The Practice of Tilling the Garden

1. Martin Luther, *The Blessed Sacrament of the Holy and True Body of Christ, and the Brotherhoods*, in *Luther's Works* 35, 51–52.

2. Christianity is often criticized for taking the metaphor of the body of Christ and turning it into a spiritualized, nonmaterial entity that is concerned with personal salvation and personal spiritual needs at the expense of real bodies and their needs. Theologian Sallie McFague argues that theological and ethical thinking that has the body of God as its starting point prioritizes "hungry, homeless, or naked human beings...over the spiritual needs of the well-fed, well-housed, well-clothed sisters and brothers." Sallie McFague, *The Body of God: An Ecological Theology* (Minneapolis: Fortress Press, 1993), 48.

Sharing the properties of Christ's body reiterates the emphasis upon the carnality or physicality of the Christian fellowship.

3. Ibid., 113. McFague says this in the broader context of her design for ecological theology. Ecological theology articulates the creation story based on the Grand Unified Theory (of which the Big-Bang theory is part), and the Theory of Everything. The universe is seen as God's body, which evolves and provides an organic unity to all life.

4. These new properties of human existence generate the new matrix of relationships that require, for example, people's dominance and exploitation of nature in order to survive or dependence of one on the others for the same reason. (The latter is not necessarily a negative aspect of human relationships.)

5. I concur that these verses can present a real danger to women when interpreted with discriminatory and patriarchal agendas in mind. Yet coming from Eastern Europe, I also know how the feminist rhetoric that challenges the primary nature and vocation of woman to be married, to be a mother, and to be the nurturer of her family can be hurtful to some women. Women in Slovakia, for example, both in professional and nonprofessional careers, value marriage and motherhood highly, and they tend to prefer it over a career. Some of them do not have any problem with being dependent on their husbands; on the contrary, they see a woman's independence as going against a woman's natural emotional composition. Slovak sociologists say, for example, "Marriage and family have held and still hold a high value with the Slovak people. Statistically, 90 percent of people get married at least once in their life and the majority of women choose to become mothers." See B. Bodnárová and J. Filadelfiová, "Deti, mládež, rodina a spoločnosť' " in *Mládež a Spoločnosť'* (Youth and Society) 7, no. 2 (2001): 16–25.

6. E. A. Speiser, *Genesis*, The Anchor Bible (New York: Doubleday, 1985), xxvii.

7. According to theorists of human development like Freud, Erikson, Gilligan, etc., these tendencies result from a differentiation and identification phase of an Oedipal child (three to five years old). It is during this period that a child identifies with the same- sex adult (ideally a parent) in order to learn intimacy with the opposite sex. The experience of undifferentiated unity with her mother is for a little girl preserved longer than it is for a boy. A girl's less radical break with

the same-sex parent (that is, her mother) enables her to see intimacy as an organic part of her personality. For a little boy, learning how to be intimate with the opposite sex is much more traumatizing. A boy experiences aggression in the process of surrendering his original oneness with his mother in order to identify with his father. This aggression becomes a male's mode of being, and it plays out as initiative, curiosity (Erikson), or a conquering, pioneering mentality.

8. Although God used material from man's body, it was God's own work of creating and molding that gave the woman her shape and life.

9. Dan McAdams, Holly Hart, and Shadd Maruna, "The Anatomy of Generativity," in *Generativity and Adult Development: How and Why We Care for the Next Generation,* ed. Dan McAdams and Ed de St. Aubin (Washington, D.C.: American Psychological Association, 1998), 10.

10. Andrea S. Taylor, "Generativity and Adult Development: Implications for Mobilizing Volunteers in Support of Youth," in *Mobilizing Adults for Positive Youth Development: Strategies for Closing the Gap between Beliefs and Behaviors,* ed. E. G. Clary and J. E. Rhodes (New York: Springer, 2006), 89.

11. Ibid.

12. Erik H. Erikson, *Identity and the Life Cycle* (New York: W. W. Norton, 1980), 103.

13. Ibid.

14. Dan McAdams, *The Redemptive Self: Stories Americans Live By* (New York: Oxford University Press, 2006), 53.

15. David White, *Practicing Discernment with Youth: A Transformative Youth Ministry Approach* (Cleveland: Pilgrim Press, 2005), 15.

16. Ibid., 16.

17. David Dollahite, Brent Slife, and Alan Hawkins, "Family Generativity and Generative Counseling: Helping Families Keep Faith with the Next Generation," in *Generativity and Adult Development,* 463.

18. McAdams, *The Redemptive Self,* 86.

19. Ibid., 85.

20. McAdams has linked generativity of persons to a particular pattern of narrating their lives. Generative people tell their life stories in redemptive terms. These stories, says McAdams, "affirm hope for the

future and a belief in human progress." See McAdams, *The Redemptive Self*, 17.

21. Dori Baker, *Doing Girlfriend Theology: God-Talk with Young Women* (Cleveland: Pilgrim Press, 2005), 116.

22. Maxine Greene, *Releasing the Imagination: Essays on Education, the Arts, and Social Change* (San Francisco: Jossey-Bass, 1995), 28.

23. Psychologist Dan McAdams cites the stories of Holocaust survivors who truthfully did not see anything transformative coming out of the atrocities that they witnessed in the concentration camps. See McAdams, *The Redemptive Self*, 259–67. An authentic search for redeeming divine presence has to be accompanied by the following set of questions: Can the face of the human soul be always transfigured after agonizing suffering? Are we pushing imagination too far when attempting to see transformative patterns behind every act of evil? May it not be holier to pay respect to pain with silence than overcome it with explanations?

24. The name and the location have been changed to protect the person's privacy.

Chapter 5: The Practice of Sharing Commons

1. Sharon D. Parks, *Big Questions, Worthy Dreams: Mentoring Young Adults in Their Search for Meaning, Purpose, and Faith* (San Francisco: Jossey-Bass, 2000), 10, 156.

2. Ibid., 10.

3. The strengths and weaknesses of the paternalism concept as applied to children and youth are discussed richly, for example, in the context of children's rights and child labor developments. Here the European and North American perspectives are challenged by Asian, Latin American, and African communities. Youth from the industrialized developed regions of the Western hemisphere, protected by child labor laws, are viewed as patronized.

4. Tina M. Durand and M. Brinton Lykes, "Think Globally, Act Locally: A Global Perspective on Mobilizing Adults for Positive Youth Development," in *Mobilizing Adults for Positive Youth Development: Strategies for Closing the Gap between Beliefs and Behaviors*, ed. E. Gil Clary and Jean E. Rhodes (New York: Springer, 2006), 239.

5. David White, *Practicing Discernment with Youth: A Trans-formative Youth Ministry Approach* (Cleveland: Pilgrim Press, 2005), 49.

6. I am not denying the existence of distinctive characteristics that accompany the adolescent stage. Yet I wish to acknowledge the cultural influences that bear on the categories and coalesce them with the roles that different cultures have for their coming-of-age populations. A helpful essay on the global diversification of the categories is Tina M. Durand and M. Brinton Lykes, "Think Globally, Act Locally: A Global Perspective on Mobilizing Adults for Positive Youth Development," in *Mobilizing Adults for Positive Youth Development, 233–54.*

7. Wanda Mitchell, "The Bathroom Mirror," in *Chicken Soup for the Soul: Grand and Great: Grandparents and Grandchildren Share Their Stories of Love and Wisdom,* ed. Jack Canfield, Mark V. Hansen, and Amy Newmark (Cos Cob, Conn.: Chicken Soup for the Soul Publishing, 2008), 17.

8. E. Gil Clary and Jean E. Rhodes, eds., "Introduction and Conceptual Foundations," in *Mobilizing Adults for Positive Youth Development,* 2.

9. Peter C. Scales, "The World of Adults Today: Implications for positive Youth Development," *Mobilizing Adults for Positive Youth Development,* 43.

10. David A. Stoddard, *The Heart of Mentoring: Ten Proven Principles for Developing People to Their Fullest Potential* (Colorado Springs, Colo.: Navpress, 2003), 50.

11. Throughout his ministry Jesus had meals with people from across the social and economic spectrum. These acts became means of Jesus' radical proclamation of the Kingdom of God by virtue of *demonstrating* the values of the inclusiveness, forgiveness, and equality. After Jesus' death, his followers would continue practicing inclusiveness through meals because this shared hospitality was seen as an integral practice for spreading and teaching Jesus' message. Many biblical scholars support this argument. I drew on the scholarship of Reta Halteman Finger, *Of Widows and Meals: Communal Meals in the Book of Acts* (Grand Rapids, Mich.: Eerdmans, 2007). Her work and the work of others affirm my argument that it was through such practices that Jesus taught and formed his followers in a distinctive way of life. I am also intrigued by the fact that what the church instituted as sacraments

or practices of faith (e.g., Eucharist, washing the feet) functioned as customary rhythms of people's lives during Jesus' time.

12. Craig Dykstra, *Growing in the Life of Faith: Education and Christian Practices,* 2nd ed. (Louisville: Westminster John Knox Press, 2005), 69.

13. I borrow the language of reconfiguration from Elizabeth Newman's discussion of liturgy as a playful act. See Elizabeth Newman, *Untamed Hospitality: Welcoming God and Other Strangers* (Grand Rapids, Mich.: Brazos Press, 2007), 158–62.

Chapter 6: To What End?

1. Martin Luther, *Judgment of Martin Luther on Monastic Vows,* in *Luther's Works* 44, 298.

2. Craig Dykstra, *Growing in the Life of Christian Faith: A Report Approved by the 201st General Assembly (1989) Presbyterian Church [U.S.A.]* (Louisville: Theology and Worship Ministry Unit, Presbyterian Church [U.S.A.], 1991), 25.

3. Ibid., 26.

4. Craig Dykstra, *Growing in the Life of Faith: Education and Christian Practices,* 2nd ed. (Louisville: Westminster John Knox Press, 2005), 66.

Bibliography

Adams, Kate, Brendan Hyde, and Richard Wooley. *The Spiritual Dimension of Childhood*. London: Jessica Kingsley Publishers, 2008.

Alexander, Christopher. *A Pattern Language: Towns, Buildings, Construction*. New York: Oxford University Press, 1977.

Allen, Holly Catterton, ed. *Nurturing Children's Spirituality: Christian Perspectives and Best Practices*. Eugene, Ore.: Cascade Books, 2008.

Anderson, Herbert, Don Browning, Ian Evison, and Mary Stewart Van Leeuwen, eds. *The Family Handbook*. Louisville: Westminster John Knox Press, 1998.

Anthony, Michael J., ed. *Perspectives on Children's Spiritual Formation*. Nashville: B &H Publishing Group, 2006.

Aquinas, Thomas. *God's Greatest Gifts: Commentaries on the Commandments and the Sacraments*. Trans. Joseph B. Collins. Manchester, N.H.: Sophia Institute Press, 1992.

———. *Summa Theologiae: A Concise Translation*. Ed. Timothy McDermott. Allen, Tex.: Christian Classics, 1989.

Arthur, Sarah. *The God-Hungry Imagination: The Art of Storytelling for Postmodern Youth Ministry*. Nashville: Upper Room Books, 2007.

Arzola, Fernando. *Toward a Prophetic Youth Ministry: Theory and Praxis in Urban Context*. Downers Grove, Ill.: InterVarsity Press, 2008.

Baker, Grinenko Dori. *Doing Girlfriend Theology: God-Talk with Young Women*. Cleveland: Pilgrim Press, 2005.

Baker, Grinenko Dori, and Joyce A. Mercer. *Lives to Offer: Accompanying Youth on their Vocational Quest*. Cleveland: Pilgrim Press, 2007.

Bakke, Timothy O. *The Best of Signature Kitchens*. Upper Saddle River, N.J.: Creative Homeowner, 2005.

Bass, Dorothy C., ed. *Practicing Our Faith: A Way of Life for a Searching People.* San Francisco: Jossey-Bass, 1997.

———. *Receiving the Day: Christian Practices for Opening the Gift of Time.* San Francisco: Jossey-Bass, 2000.

Bausch, William J. *Storytelling, Imagination and Faith.* Mystic, Conn.: Twenty-Third Publications, 1984.

Beckwith, Ivy. *Formational Children's Ministry: Shaping Children Using Story, Ritual, and Relationship.* Grand Rapids, Mich.: Baker Books, 2010.

Bennethum, Michael D. *Listen! God Is Calling! Luther Speaks of Vocation, Faith, and Work.* Minneapolis: Augsburg Fortress, 2003.

Benson, Peter L., Eugene C. Roehlkepartain, and Kathryn L. Hong, eds. *Spiritual Development: New Directions for Youth Development.* San Francisco: Jossey-Bass, 2008.

Berryman, Jerome W. *Children and the Theologians: Clearing the Way for Grace.* Harrisburg, Pa.: Morehouse Publishing, 2009.

Blum-Kulka, Shoshana. *Dinner Talk: Cultural Patterns of Sociability and Socialization in Family Discourse.* Mahwah, N.J.: Lawrence Erlbaum Associates, Inc., 1997.

Bodnárová, Božena, and Jarmila Filadelfiová. "Deti, mládež, rodina a spoločnosť'." In *Mládež a Spoločnosť'* (Youth and Society) 7, no. 2 (2001): 16–25.

Browning, Don S. *Equality and the Family: A Fundamental, Practical Theology of Children.* Grand Rapids, Mich.: Eerdmans, 2007.

Bugeja, Michael. *Interpersonal Divide: The Search for Community in a Technological Age.* New York: Oxford University Press, 2005.

Caldwell, Elizabeth F. *Making a Home for Faith: Nurturing the Spiritual Life of Your Children.* Cleveland: Pilgrim Press, 2000.

Chodorow, Nancy J. *Feminism and Psychoanalytic Theory.* New Haven, Conn.: Yale University Press, 1989.

Clark, Chap. *Hurt. Inside the World of Today's Teenagers.* Grand Rapids, Mich.: Baker Academic, 2004.

Clark, Chap, and Dee Clark. *Disconnected: Parenting Teens in a MySpace World.* Grand Rapids, Mich.: Baker Books, 2007.

Clary, E. Gil, and Jean E. Rhodes. "Introduction and Conceptual Foundations." In *Mobilizing Adults for Positive Youth Development: Strategies for Closing the Gap between Beliefs and Behaviors.* Ed. E. Gil Clary and Jean E. Rhodes. New York: Springer, 2006.

Conran, Terence. *Kitchens: The Hub of the Home.* New York: Clarkson Potter Publisher, 2002.

"Crime." Posted online at *www.cnn.com/2008/CRIME/11/21/webcam .suicide/index.html.* Accessed on November 22, 2008.

Damon, William. *The Path to Purpose: How Young People Find Their Calling in Life.* New York: Free Press, 2008.

Darwin, Charles. *The Origin of Species.* New York: Gramercy Books, 1979.

Dean, Kenda C. *Practicing Passion: Youth and the Quest for a Passionate Church.* Grand Rapids, Mich.: Eerdmans, 2004.

Dean, Kenda C., and Richard R. Osmer. *Youth, Religion and Globalization.* Zurich: LIT Verlag, 2007.

DesCombes, Joan. "2008 NKBA Design Competition Winners." In *National Kitchen and Bath Association.* Posted at *www.nkba.org/consumer_inspiration_2008_dc_winners.aspx.* Accessed on October 27, 2008.

DeVries, Mark. *Family-Based Youth Ministry.* Downers Grove, Ill.: InterVarsity Press, 1994.

———. *Sustainable Youth Ministry: Why Most Youth Ministry Doesn't Last and What Your Church Can Do about It.* Downers Grove, Ill.: InterVarsity Press, 2008.

Dollahite, David, Brent Slife, and Alan Hawkins. "Family Generativity and Generative Counseling: Helping Families Keep Faith with the Next Generation." In *Generativity and Adult Development,* ed. Dan McAdams and Ed de St. Aubin. Washington, D.C.: American Psychology Association Publications, 1998.

Durand, Tina M., and M. Brinton Lykes. "Think Globally, Act Locally: A Global Perspective on Mobilizing Adults for Positive Youth Development." In *Mobilizing Adults for Positive Youth Development: Strategies for Closing the Gap between Beliefs and Behaviors.* Ed. E. Gil Clary and Jean E. Rhodes. New York: Springer, 2006.

Dykstra, Craig. *Growing in the Life of Faith. Education and Christian Practices.* Louisville: Westminster John Knox Press, 2005.

———. *Growing in the Life of Christian Faith: A Report Approved by the 201st General Assembly (1989) Presbyterian Church (U.S.A.).* USA: Theology and Worship Ministry Unit, Presbyterian Church (U.S.A.), 1991.

Dykstra, Robert C., Allan Hugh Coles, Jr., and Donald Capps. *Losers, Loners, and Rebels: The Spiritual Struggles of Boys*. Louisville: Westminster John Knox Press, 2007.

Eaude, T. *Children's Spiritual, Moral, Social and Cultural Development — Primary and Early Years*. 2nd ed. Exeter, UK: Learning Matters, 2008.

Edie, Fred P. *Book, Bath, Table, and Time. Christian Worship as Source and Resource for Youth Ministry*. Cleveland: Pilgrim Press, 2007.

Elkind, David. *The Hurried Child. Growing Up Too Fast Too Soon*. 3rd ed. New York: Da Capo Press, 2001.

Erikson, Erik H. *Identity and the Life Cycle*. New York: W. W. Norton, 1980.

Estep, James, Michael Anthony, and Greg Allison. *A Theology for Christian Education*. Nashville: B &H Publishing Group, 2008.

Everist, Norma Cook. *Open the Doors and See All the People: Stories of Congregational Identity and Vocation*. Minneapolis: Augsburg Fortress, 2005.

Finger, Reta Halteman. *Of Widows and Meals: Communal Meals in the Book of Acts*. Grand Rapids, Mich.: Eerdmans, 2007.

Folmsbee, Chris. *A New Kind of Youth Ministry*. Grand Rapids, Mich.: Zondervan Publishing Company, 2007.

Fosarelli, Patricia D. *ASAP: Ages, Stages and Phases: From Infancy to Adolescence; Integrating Physical, Social, Emotional, Intellectual, and Spiritual Development*. Ligouri, Mo.: Ligouri Press, 2006.

Fowler, James W. *Stages of Faith: The Psychology of Human Development and the Quest for Meaning*. San Francisco: HarperSanFrancisco, 1995.

Freud, Sigmund. *The Ego and the Id*. New York: W. W. Norton, 1960.
———. *Three Contributions to the Theory of Sex*. Trans. A. A. Brill. Stilwell, Kans.: Digireads Publishing, 2008.

Gillespie, Shay. *...And a Little Child Shall Lead Them...Spiritual and Straight-up Childcare for Right Now*. Bloomington, Ind.: Universe, 2006.

Gilligan, Carol. *In a Different Voice: Psychological Theory and Women's Development*. Cambridge, Mass.: Harvard University Press, 1982.

Gilligan, Carol, and David A. J. Richards. *The Deepening Darkness: Patriarchy, Resistance, and Democracy's Future*. New York: Cambridge University Press, 2009.

Gordon, Cynthia. "Al Gore's Our Guy: Linguistically Constructing a Family Political Identity." In *Family Talk: Discourse and Identity in Four American Families,* ed. D. Tannen, S. Kendall, and C. Gordon, 233–63. New York: Oxford University Press, 2007.

Greene, Maxine. *Releasing the Imagination: Essays on Education, the Arts and Social Change.* San Francisco: Jossey-Bass, 1995.

Grimbol, William R. *Jesus in Your Backpack: A Teen's Guide to Spiritual Wisdom.* Berkley, Calif.: Ulysses Press, 2007.

Habermas, Ronald T. *Introduction to Christian Education Formation: A Lifelong Plan for Christ-Centered Restoration.* New York: HarperCollins, 2008.

Heflin, Houston. *Youth Pastor: The Theology and Practice of Youth Ministry.* Nashville: Abingdon Press, 2009.

Heischman, Daniel R. *Good Influence: Teaching the Wisdom of Adulthood.* Harrisburg, Pa.: Morehouse Publishing, 2009.

Hendricks, Patricia. *Hungry Souls, Holy Companions: Mentoring a New Generation of Christians.* Harrisburg, Pa.: Morehouse Publishing, 2006.

Hersch, Patricia. *A Tribe Apart: A Journey into the Heart of American Adolescence.* New York: Ballantine Books, 1998.

Hess, Lakey Carol. *Caretakers of Our Common House: Women's Development in Communities of Faith.* Nashville: Abingdon Press, 1997.

———. "Ministry with Children and Youth." In *The Family Handbook,* ed. Herbert Anderson, Don Browning, Ian Evison, and Mary Stewart Van Leeuwen, 132–37. Louisville: Westminster John Knox Press, 1998.

hooks, bell. *Yearning: Race, Gender, and Cultural Politics.* Boston, Mass.: South End Press, 1990.

Hyde, B. *Children and Spirituality: Searching for Meaning and Connectedness.* London: Jessica Kingsley Publishers, 2008.

"In Lean Times, Comfort in a Bountiful Meal." Posted at *www.nytimes.com/2008/11/28/us/28thanks.html?emc=eta1.* Accessed on November 28, 2008.

Isay, Dave. *Listening Is an Act of Love: A Celebration of American Life from the StoryCorps Project.* New York: Penguin Press, 2007.

Jackson, Maggie. *What's Happening to Home? Balancing Work, Life, and Refuge in the Information Age.* Notre Dame, Ind.: Sorin Books, 2002.

Jones, Tony. *The Sacred Way*. Grand Rapids, Mich.: Zondervan Publishing Company, 2009.

Jung, Shannon L. *Food for Life: The Spirituality and Ethics of Eating*. Minneapolis: Fortress Press, 2004.

Kaufman, Gordon D. *The Theological Imagination: Constructing the Concept of God*. Philadelphia: Westminster Press, 1981.

Keeley, Robert. *Helping Our Children Grow in Faith: How the Church Can Nurture the Spiritual Development of Kids*. Grand Rapids, Mich.: Baker Press, 2008.

Kendall, Peggy. *Connected: Christian Parenting in an Age of IM and MySpace*. Valley Forge, Pa.: Judson Press, 2007.

———. *Rewired: Youth Ministry in an Age of IM and MySpace*. Valley Forge, Pa.: Judson Press, 2007.

Kennedy, Tracy L. M., Aaron Smith, Amy Tracy Wells, and Barry Wellman. *Pew Internet and American Life Project. Networked Families*. Posted at *www.pewinternet.org*. Accessed on November 12, 2008.

King, Mike. *Presence-Centered Youth Ministry. Guiding Students into Spiritual Formation*. Downers Grove, Ill.: InterVarsity Press, 2006.

Kizinna, Doris. *Go Deep: Spiritual Practices for Youth Ministry*. Kelona, B.C., Canada: Wood Lake Publishing, Inc., 2009.

Lenhart, Amanda. "Cyberbullying and Online Teens." In *Pew Internet & American Life Project*. Posted at *www.pewinternet.org/pdfs/PIP%20Cyberbullying%20Memo; pdf*. Accessed on November 12, 2008.

Loder, James E. *The Logic of the Spirit: Human Development in Theological Perspective*. San Francisco: Jossey Bass, 1998.

Long, Thomas G. *Testimony: Talking Ourselves into Being Christian*. San Francisco: Jossey-Bass, 2004.

Lovett, Maney Susan. *The Smart Approach to Kitchen Design*. 3rd ed. Upper Saddle River, N.J.: Creative Homeowner, 2006.

Luther Seminary and Southwestern Seminary. "Factors in Youth and Young Adult Faith. Experience and Development: A Longitudinal Study." Posted at *www.faithfactors.com/docs/Longdt.doc*. Accessed on October 23, 2006.

Luther, Martin. "The Judgment of Martin Luther on Monastic Vows." In *Luther's Works*. Vol. 44. Ed. James Atkinson and Helmut T. Lehmann, 243–400. Trans. James Atkinson. Philadelphia: Fortress Press, 1966.

————. "The Blessed Sacrament of the Holy and True Body of Christ, and the Brotherhoods." In *Luther's Works.* Vol. 35. Ed. Theodore E. Bachmann, 45–75. Trans. Jeremiah Schindel. Philadelphia: Muhlenberg Press, 1960.

Lyons, Patricia. *The Soul of Adolescence: In Their Own Words.* Harrisburg, Pa.: Morehouse Publishing, 2010.

Macgill, Alexandra Rankin. "Parents, Teens and Technology." In PewResearch Center Publications. Posted at *www.pewresearch.org/pubs/621/parents-teens-and-technology.* Accessed on November 12, 2008.

Mahan, Brian J. *Forgetting Ourselves on Purpose: Vocation and the Ethics of Ambition.* San Francisco: Jossey-Bass, 2002.

Mahan, Brian J., Michael Warren, and David F. White. *Awakening Youth Discipleship.* Eugene, Ore.: Cascade Publishing, 2008.

Maiko, Saneta. *Youth, Faith and Culture: Contemporary Theories and Practices of Youth Ministry.* Bloomington, Ind.: AuthorHouse, 2007.

McAdams, Dan. *The Redemptive Self: Stories Americans Live By.* New York: Oxford University Press, 2006.

McAdams, Dan, Holly Hart, and Shadd Maruna. "The Anatomy of Generativity." In *Generativity and Adult Development: How and Why We Care for the Next Generation.* Ed. Dan McAdams and Ed de St. Aubin. Washington, D.C.: American Psychological Association, 1998.

McFague, Sallie. *The Body of God: An Ecological Theology.* Minneapolis: Fortress Press, 1993.

Mercer, Joyce A. *Welcoming Children: A Practical Theology of Childhood.* St. Louis: Chalice Press, 2005.

Miller-McLemore, Bonnie J. *In the Midst of Chaos: Caring for Children as Spiritual Practice.* San Francisco: Jossey-Bass, 2007.

Mitchell, Wanda. "The Bathroom Mirror." In *Chicken Soup for the Soul: Grand and Great. Grandparents and Grandchildren Share Their Stories of Love and Wisdom,* ed. Jack Canfield, Mark V. Hansen, and Amy Newmark, 17–20. Cos Cob, Conn.: Chicken Soup for the Soul Publishing, 2008.

Moore, Mary Elizabeth. *Teaching as a Sacramental Act.* Cleveland: Pilgrim Press, 2004.

————. *Teaching from the Heart: Theology and Educational Method.* Harrisburg, Pa.: Trinity Press International, 1998.

Moore, Mary Elizabeth, and Almeda Wright, eds. *Children, Youth, and Spirituality in a Troubling World*. St. Louis: Chalice Press, 2008.

Morey, Tim. *Embodying Our Faith: Becoming a Living, Sharing, Practicing Church*. Downers Grove, Ill.: InterVarsity Press, 2009.

Mueller, Walt. *Engaging the Soul of Youth Culture: Bridging Teen Worldviews and Christian Truth*. Downers Grove, Ill.: InterVarsity Press, 2006.

National Center on Addiction and Substance Abuse at Columbia University. Posted at *www.casacolumbia.org/absolutenm/articlefiles/380–Importance%20of%20Family%20Diners%20IV.pdf*. Accessed on March 11, 2008.

Neafsey John. *A Sacred Voice Is Calling: Personal Vocation and Social Conscience*. Maryknoll, N.Y.: Orbis Books, 2006.

Newman, Elizabeth. *Untamed Hospitality: Welcoming God and Other Strangers*. Grand Rapids, Mich.: Brazos Press, 2007.

O'Brien, Maureen. "How We Are Together: Educating for Group Self-Understanding in the Congregation." In *Religious Education* 92, no. 3 (1997): 315–22.

Oestreicher, Mark. *Youth Ministry 3.0.: A Manifesto of Where We've Been, Where We Are, and Where We Need to Go*. Grand Rapids, Mich.: Zondervan Publishing Company, 2008.

Osmer, Richard R. *Confirmation: Presbyterian Practices in Ecumenical Perspective*. Louisville: Geneva Press, 1996.

Ota, Cathy, and Mark Chater. *Spiritual Education in a Divided World: Social, Environmental, and Pedagogical Perspectives on the Spirituality of Children and Young People*. London: Taylor and Francis, 2007.

Parks, Sharon D. *Big Questions, Worthy Dreams: Mentoring Young Adults in Their Search for Meaning, Purpose, and Faith*. San Francisco: Jossey-Bass, 2000.

———. "Home and Pilgrimage: Companion Metaphors for Personal and Social Transformation." *Soundings* 72, nos. 2–3 (Summer–Fall 1989): 304. Quoted in Elizabeth F. Caldwell. *Making a Home for Faith: Nurturing the Spiritual Life of Your Children*. Cleveland: Pilgrim Press, 2000.

———. "Household Economics." In *Practicing Our Faith: A Way of Life for a Searching People*, ed. Dorothy C. Bass, 43–59. San Francisco: Jossey-Bass, 1997.

Parker, Evelyn. "Theological Framework for Youth Ministry: Hope." In *Starting Right: Thinking Theologically about Youth Ministry,* ed. Kenda C. Dean, Chap Clark, and David Rahn, 265–76. Grand Rapids, Mich.: Zondervan Publishing Company, 2001.

Paulsell, Stephanie. *Honoring the Body: Meditations on a Christian Practice.* San Francisco: Jossey-Bass, 2002.

Peterson-LaCelle, Kristina. *Liberating Tradition: Women's Identity in Christian Perspective.* Grand Rapids, Mich.: Baker Academic, 2008.

Pettegree, Andrew. *Reformation and the Culture of Persuasion.* New York: Cambridge University Press, 2005.

Placher, William C., ed. *Callings: Twenty Centuries of Christian Wisdom on Vocation.* Grand Rapids, Mich.: Eerdmans, 2005.

Plotkin, Bill. *Nature and the Human Soul: Cultivating Wholeness and Community in a Fragmented World.* Novato, Calif.: New World Library, 2008.

Pollan, Michael. *In Defense of Food: An Eater's Manifesto.* New York: Penguin Press, 2008.

Putnam, Robert D. *Bowling Alone: The Collapse and Revival of American Community.* New York: Simon and Schuster, 2000.

Putnam, Robert D., and Lewis M. Feldstein. *Better Together: Restoring American Community.* New York: Simon & Schuster, 2003.

Ricoeur, Paul. *History and Truth.* Trans. Charles A. Kelbley. Evanston, Ill.: Northwestern University Press, 1965.

Riera, Michael. *Staying Connected to Your Teenager: How to Keep Them Talking to You and How to Hear What They're Really Saying.* Cambridge, Mass.: Perseus Publishing, 2003.

Root, Andrew. *Revising Relational Youth Ministry: From a Strategy of Influence to a Theology of Incarnation.* Downers Grove, Ill.: InterVarsity Press, 2007.

Russell, Letty M. *Church in the Round: Feminist Interpretation of the Church.* Louisville: Westminster John Knox Press, 1993.

Scales, Peter C. "The World of Adults Today: Implications for Positive Youth Development." In *Mobilizing Adults for Positive Youth Development: Strategies for Closing the Gap between Beliefs and Behaviors.* Ed. E. Gil Clary and Jean E. Rhodes. New York: Springer, 2006.

Schoor, Verni. *Compass. A Guide for Character and Spiritual Formation in Children.* Erie, Colo.: Character Choice, 2008.

Schultze, Quentin J. *Habits of the High-Tech Heart: Living Virtuously in the Information Age.* Grand Rapids, Mich.: Baker Academic, 2002.

Schwehn, Mark R., and Dorothy C. Bass. *Leading Lives That Matter: What We Should Do and Who We Should Be.* Grand Rapids, Mich.: Eerdmans, 2006.

Sclove, Richard E. "Making Technology Democratic." In *Resisting the Virtual Life: The Culture and Politics of Information,* ed. James Brook and Ian A. Boal, 85–105. San Francisco: City Lights, 1995.

Senter, Mark. *When God Shows Up: A History of Protestant Youth Ministry in America.* Grand Rapids, Mich.: Baker Books, 2010.

Shapiro, H. Svi. *Losing Heart: The Moral and Spiritual Mis-education of America's Children.* Mahwah, N.J.: Lawrence Erlbaum Associates, 2006.

Smith, Preserved. *Luther's Table Talk: A Critical Study.* New York: AMS Press, 1907.

Souza, M., Leslie J. Francis, James O'Higgins-Norman, and Daniel G. Scott, eds. *International Handbook of Education for Spirituality, Care, and Wellbeing.* Dordrecht, The Netherlands: Springer Academic Publishers, 2009.

Speiser, E. A. *Genesis.* The Anchor Bible. New York: Doubleday & Company, Inc., 1985.

Stoddard, David A. *The Heart of Mentoring: Ten Proven Principles for Developing People to Their Fullest Potential.* Colorado Springs, Colo.: Navpress, 2003.

Stonehouse, Catherine, and Scottie May. *Listening to Children on the Spiritual Journey.* Grand Rapids, Mich.: Baker Publishing, 2010.

Strauss, Gerald. *Luther's House of Learning: Indoctrination of the Young in the German Reformation.* Baltimore: Johns Hopkins University Press, 1978.

Tannen, Deborah. *Gender and Discourse.* New York: Oxford University Press, 1996.

———. *You're Wearing That? Understanding Mothers and Daughters in Conversation.* New York: Random House, 2006.

Tapscott, Don. *Growing Up Digital: The Rise of the Net Generation.* New York: McGraw-Hill, 1998.

Taylor, Andrea S. "Generativity and Adult Development: Implications for Mobilizing Volunteers in Support of Youth." In *Mobilizing Adults for Positive Youth Development: Strategies for Closing the*

Gap between Beliefs and Behaviors. Ed. E. G. Clary and J. E. Rhodes. New York: Springer, 2006.

Taylor, Barry. *Entertainment Theology: New Edge Spirituality in a Digital Democracy.* Grand Rapids, Mich.: Baker Academic, 2008.

Traina, Cristina L. H. "A Person in the Making." In *The Child in Christian Thought,* ed. Marcia J. Bunge, 103–33. Grand Rapids, Mich.: Eerdmans, 2001.

Troland, Tom. "Homesight: The Five Stages of Kitchen Remodeling." In *National Kitchen and Bath Association.* Posted at *www.nkba.org/consumer_tools_statistics.aspx.* Accessed on October 23, 2008.

Turpin, Katherine. *Branded: Adolescents Converting from Consumer Faith.* Cleveland: Pilgrim Press, 2006.

Ulanov, Ann Belford. *Receiving Woman: Studies in the Psychology and Theology of the Feminine.* Philadelphia: Westminster Press, 1981.

Volf, Miroslav, and Dorothy C. Bass, eds. *Practicing Theology. Beliefs and Practices in Christian Life.* Grand Rapids, Mich.: Eerdmans, 2002.

Ward, Pete. *Liquid Church.* Peabody, Mass.: Hendrickson Publishers, 2002.

Weinstein, Miriam. *The Surprising Power of Family Meals: How Eating Together Makes Us Smarter, Stronger, Healthier, and Happier.* Hanover, N.H.: Steerforth Press, 2005.

White, David. *Practicing Discernment with Youth: A Transformative Youth Ministry Approach.* Cleveland: Pilgrim Press, 2005.

Wilhoit, James. *Spiritual Formation as if the Church Mattered. Growing in Christ Through Community.* Grand Rapids, Mich.: Baker Academic, 2008.

Yaconelli, Mark. *Downtime. Helping Teenagers Pray.* New York: HarperCollins, 2008.